TRINF
PUBLIS

SPIRITUAL CONVERSATIONS
WITH A SKEPTIC

**On God Consciousness
and The Absolute**

BENTINHO MASSARO

EDITED BY LISA RAPP

Spiritual Conversations with a Skeptic
On God Consciousness and The Absolute

BentinhoMassaro.com

Trinfinity Publishing, London UK
ISBN 978-0-578-64924-5

Editing & book design by Lisa Rapp
Cover art by Cory Katuna
Transcription by Gail Holwell & Gloria Vigneault

Who you are cannot be put into words. When the concept-ridden mind subsides, the Light of the Infinite begins to shine through. Once this Light or Awareness is sufficiently aligned to, words are no longer for you; they are merely tools to assist others in awakening to the Infinite within.

~ Bentinho Massaro

TABLE OF CONTENTS

Preface   1

Foreword by Russell   5

Introduction by Bentinho   9

Conversation 1:
Creation, Awareness & Infinite Reality   19

Conversation 2:
Deeper into Infinite Reality   77

Conversation 3:
Perception, Truth & Levels of Consciousness   111

About the Author   157

Resources   159

PREFACE

Spiritual Conversations with a Skeptic was born of an unlikely friendship between spiritual teacher, Bentinho Massaro, and "Russell" (a pseudonym), a semi-retired neurologist and one of Bentinho's close friends. The two have known each other for several years, and from time to time, get together to enjoy a good cigar, a bit of scotch and a lively discussion on any number of topics. At a certain point, they decided to record some of their dialogues. This book (and potential future volumes) is the result.

I have called this "an unlikely friendship" because, at first glance, one would not anticipate such close rapport between two people of such widely divergent backgrounds and interests, as well as nearly opposite philosophical views on "the nature of reality." Bentinho has dedicated the better part of his 31 years to experientially exploring the capabilities and workings of the human mind, consciousness, metaphysics, as well as the nature of God and the many different paths to Enlightenment (mostly the direct paths). He has committed himself to distilling these different teachings in ways that are relevant, experiential and accessible to humanity in today's modern age. For over 10 years now, Bentinho has been teaching his unique and comprehensive synthesis of spirituality to audiences around the world.

In contrast, Russell, who is a scientist by nature and training, has adopted a more material-based worldview and considers himself a "skeptic" when it comes to matters of spirituality and metaphysics. Whereas Bentinho believes, and claims to experience, that "the world" (as in "the universe") exists inside of the reality of consciousness as perception only, Russell adheres to the more traditional Western viewpoint of an empirically existent, or objective, universe or reality. He views consciousness as a product of matter or of the world; or more specifically, as a phenomenon produced by the brain.

Despite these fundamental differences in perception, a friendship between the two developed and has persisted, perhaps due to their shared enjoyment of intellectual dialectic (with a few jokes and a lot of laughter thrown in), as well a mutual respect and allowance for each other's viewpoints and intelligence. Neither display any need to be right and prove the other wrong. As a result, these dialogues radiate light-heartedness throughout, even while the subject matter is substantial.

In the conversations presented here, Bentinho and Russell dive right in, exploring and questioning each other's views and understandings about reality in a playful, yet thoughtful and deliberate way. Bentinho's answers to Russell's questions often expand into subtle intellectual and experiential territories, for example, his proposition that an individual has the intrinsic ability to realize that which exists beyond even God: The Absolute, or the One

Infinite Source. Depending on the reader's background, this perspective, as well as others presented here, may seem a bit "unorthodox." But for those who approach these teachings with an open mind, seeking to penetrate beyond their current level of awareness and understanding, much will be gained from these conversations.

Suffice it to say that this is highly subtle material for even a seasoned spiritual adept, let alone a scientific-minded skeptic! So, cheers to Russell, whose open-mindedness, genuine curiosity and sound reasoning skills lead him to persist in these explorations, and to Bentinho for his skillful guidance and clear pointing to that which eternally exists beyond the grasp of the mind.

Enjoy!
Lisa Rapp, Editor

FOREWORD BY RUSSELL

I'm a 62-year-old, semi-retired neurologist who has been studying philosophy and thinking about big philosophical questions for about a year. Maybe this is because I'm starting to realize my age, or maybe it's because I finally have some free time to ponder abstract ideas, or maybe it's because I've had the pleasure to spend some time with Bentinho Massaro, a whipper-snapper just half my age.

I want to know the truth and I'm looking for answers, but I'm not yet so desperate that I must settle for answers that aren't either intuitively or analytically valid to me. I have a clear analytical bias—I enjoy chess and doing crossword puzzles and Words With Friends. For those who are familiar with the Myers-Briggs personality scale, I'm a strong "T" (Thinking). Intuition is important, and in significant ways more important than logic and reasoning, but I trust my rational brain more than my intuitive brain.

Do people have free will? What is consciousness? How do we know anything? How certain can we be of what we know, and does it matter? What is the nature of reality? What is the meaning of life? What is the right thing to do? These are questions that some of the greatest minds in history have tried to answer.

Philosophy used to include more subject matter than it does today. Many philosophers of old were leading scientists, mathematicians, physicians, lawyers, emperors and/or historians of their time.

The ancient Greek philosophers philosophized, among other things, about the nature of material things. Some thought that everything around us was made out of some combination of fire, air, water and earth. In modern times, science has convinced most everyone that there are different types of atoms that can combine to form lots of different types of molecules. So, philosophy has become smaller; philosophy textbooks today no longer discuss the composition of material things unless it's part of a discussion of the history of philosophy.

Likewise, much of astronomy is no longer up for philosophical debate. And with the research tools cognitive neuroscientists are using to explore the functioning of the human brain, I believe "consciousness" will soon join astronomy, physics and chemistry as being relatively off limits to philosophers. But that still leaves a lot to discuss!

I always enjoy chatting with Bentinho while smoking cigars and sometimes drinking whiskey or a beer. He's intelligent, charming in a way, funny, articulate, and can do more pull-ups than I can. On the other hand, I think it's fair to say that, despite my age, I'm better looking than he is (jk!) and can beat him pretty easily at basketball and pickleball (not jk!).

I'm a skeptic at heart, and though I'm fascinated by Bentinho's conception of how everything fits together, I can't buy the whole picture yet. I'm not ready to throw away my science worldview and take a mental leap that this world of ours is all an illusion. I believe I'm open to doing just that, but where's the evidence that would persuade me to do so? Give me just one good piece of evidence!

It seems the best evidence Bentinho can give me regarding "infinite reality" and the assertion that this world is an illusion is his own experience of infinite reality or oneness. I'm afraid I don't accept this evidence. Many people who take psychedelics are convinced that they've experienced universal oneness or universal love or true reality or Jesus or God. Perhaps it is reality which they are connecting to, but I'm leaning toward these experiences representing psychological phenomena that are chemically induced.

This doesn't diminish their importance (in this world, at least). As Michael Pollan suggests in his book, *How to Change Your Mind*, whether or not these experiences represent absolute reality does not reduce the significance of these experiences to the person undergoing them.

Finally, I'd like to thank Bentinho for sharing some of his time and wisdom with me. Even though some of his wisdom was probably lost on me, perhaps it will be of benefit to others. We covered a lot of ground in our discussions, but in some ways I feel like we've just scratched the surface. I sincerely hope we will have more opportunities to further our discussions, especially if he's the one supplying the cigars.

~ Russell

INTRODUCTION BY BENTINHO

Russell could be categorized as "a grounded intellectual, an atheist, a neurologist and a skeptic." I don't think he himself would disagree with any of these labels. More recently, he has developed an active and committed passion for philosophy. He is a friend of mine and exactly twice my age.

Russell is one of my favorite "3D-focused" people to interact with, as his intellectual capacity, kind-hearted spirit, inquisitive skepticism, and knowledgeable "earthly" mind always make for an enjoyable conversation in which we are able to bridge different world views. Conversing with him also allows me to more fully ground some of my concepts and visions into systems and language that could benefit or reach the portion of our collective that he eloquently represents, in an intelligible and relatable way.

We share the same kind of dry, intellectual, quick-witted humor. We sometimes beat each other to the same joke or pun and enjoy teasing each other intellectually. It's almost always fast-paced, and when we interact, half the time we both can't help but have a giddy smile on our faces.

9

I believe skepticism the world over can go through an evolution, transmuting into a more positive and holistic attitude than it typically is. I feel Russell is a potentially good and rare example of what the term "healthy skepticism" could actually hint at.

Some may disagree, but in my experience, the attitude the word "skepticism" points to is essentially a negative attitude, even when it is made to look or sound positive. Vibrationally, thus far, I have felt it to be a subtly negative approach to life. It seems to me that there is no such thing as a completely positive form of skepticism; that "positive" or "healthy" skepticism is a mislabeling of what we perhaps hope to mean by it. In my experience, even self-proclaimed "healthy skeptics" carry with them a vibration of non-wellbeing, mistrust and non-freedom. It feels more fixed and limiting than the skeptics themselves are generally able to see and admit.

The psychological root of skepticism tends to be a fear of being vulnerable, wrong or deluded, with an additional fear of being ridiculed by others, or by society at large, for being vulnerable, wrong or deluded.

Skeptics typically take pride in their intellectual prowess and their ability to have their knowledge reflect or represent in a clear way the most collectively-agreed-upon paradigm, with only a few skeptics pushing the edge of what's generally accepted.

They generally fear breaking away too far from what their society currently thinks, and therefore the speed at which they can expand their understanding of life is comparatively / relatively slow. This fear, just like any fear, is essentially a negative energy and it limits the expansion of the consciousness of the skeptic.

I respect skeptics just as I respect anyone, yet without meaning to insult anyone: I see skeptics generally as quite fearful humans; scared to be wrong and scared to be ridiculed or outed by their society. I don't think most skeptics realize how much of their motivation to be a skeptic is rooted in their fear to be wrong in the eyes of others, and therefore, how much they are holding back their own curiosity, investigations and findings by their own choice to submit to the fear of being ridiculed.

Of course there are always exceptions, but in most cases, social safety and security—provided by the respect they enjoy from their peers—seems to be one of the skeptic's main comforts and attachments. They oftentimes justify this limitation using the fact that many other sensible or realistic people—the majority of society's respected people—would agree with their views. As such, they are typically cemented in an existing paradigm or framework by their own free will; a paradigm that—like any paradigm —limits their happiness, as well as what is possible for them to realize or achieve.

Since most people already have deep doubts about themselves, their dreams, and what is possible in life, the attitude of skepticism is one that tends to easily spread and rub off on others. This is especially true for those who are less intellectually adept than the skeptics they are around. A smart skeptic's influence on those with lesser intellectual confidence can often slow down their vibration, self-confidence and self-belief, as well as their general energy level and vitality.

One of the dangers of exposing someone with self-doubt and insecurities to an intelligent skeptic is that the intellectually adept skeptic can use sound logic in practically any situation to kill a person's sense of faith in the invisible by proving things wrong, or through the use of other intellectual tactics. The intellectual can make his or her conclusions sound solid and conclusive, even when there are many holes and biases in their conclusion. They can make it sound convincing to a degree where other people will now accept the concluded limitation as true, simply because they cannot see any way to argue with it. Therefore, they take on that belief system, even if the limitation is not a fact or an absolute at all.

If one doesn't stand with true confidence in one's own sense of limitless possibilities, and a firm faith in the intuitive and the invisible aspects of life, then when there is a skeptic around, what usually happens is that one closes some inner doors through which happiness can flow— doorways that are typically kept open by the sense of "everything is possible," or similar optimistic convictions.

Almost all of those I am aware of who left a deeply positive, ground-breaking mark on this Earth, benefitting millions of lives in inspiring ways, were generally imaginative, intuitive dreamers at heart, who believed that virtually anything is possible or accomplishable. This does not mean they were not also "realistic" from time to time, but skepticism and realism were definitely not their primary foundations.

I think the only type of truly healthy skepticism is curiosity. Curiosity in its purest form is that which we see in a young child: an empty, truly open-minded attitude in which the only intention is to get to the bottom of what's going on; to experientially understand, or grok, how something operates—without bias or a predetermined mindset.

A bias can be relatively, temporarily useful, but as I have come to view biases, they are ultimately always unhealthy, low in vibration and limiting. Since skepticism is almost always wielded with the bias of skepticism itself, along with a host of conclusions and assumptions about what is factual and real, it is therefore, according to my definition, typically a somewhat unhealthy and negative attitude. It's just that most people don't realize the ongoing, subtle, detrimental energetic effects that the attitude of skepticism has on their body, mind and spirit and on those around them who they inevitably influence.

On the other hand, the truly open-minded, curious ones do not care whether their intuitive and/or intellectual findings fit into today's societal agreements or present-day understandings. Nor do they care if they fit in with their own previous findings or understandings! As such, the curious one is truly open, unlike the "healthy skeptic" who is usually quite locked into an already bought-into paradigm of assumptions that remain uninvestigated. Skeptics typically investigate things outside of their own paradigm and often forget to investigate their already existing paradigm of assumptions.

Since skepticism, by its very definition, is never unbiased, it can also never lead to truly objective results or conclusions. A skeptic may be able to arrive at a conclusion that makes sense within certain agreed upon parameters, but to believe that this means a particular mystery, phenomenon, experience or paradox has actually been fully understood is folly.

In my view, Russell sits nicely in between what most would think of as a healthy, grounded skeptic and someone who is genuinely curious. He is, in many ways, at the leading-edge of what skepticism could evolve into. This is mostly due to his balanced and open heart. He allows everyone to have their own point of view, he is not looking to convince anyone per se (if at all), and he is sincerely interested in anything that can help him expand his understanding of life and the things within it. He is genuinely caring.

Russell has the humility needed for this type of continual growth. He might find a temporary sort of satisfaction, or even a sense of fun, in intelligently proving something right or wrong, possible or impossible. But at the end of the day, he remains open to being wrong, and prefers love and respect over pride and being right. He is unusually aware of his own biases and beliefs and is able to admit them as biases and belief systems without feeling emotionally defensive of his point of view. And rather than stating them as facts or absolute truths and going to war with another's point of view, he realizes his world view is ever evolving and every assumption is up for further investigation. He typically seems unafraid to potentially have his views undermined.

Even though our paradigms are worlds apart, Russell's humility and curiosity, combined with his sense of humor, intelligence and kind heart, makes it a true joy to interact with him! Our relationship is a good example of how people from entirely different paradigms the world over can not only get along and tolerate each other, but can even have very fruitful and enjoyable relationships and interactions and co-create things that can be of help in society.

Another thing I very much appreciate about Russell is that our interactions allow me to refine and bridge some of my philosophy and vision of a happier civilization for all. An intention which Russell seems to passionately share, by the way.

And so, any time I happen to be in the neighborhood, we usually spend a few hours by ourselves enjoying a cigar and some scotch, letting the conversation naturally unfold. We have come to expect good dialogue, I think, and therefore it generally happens.

Most often our conversations are about philosophy and spirituality, new governmental and architectural structures for an improved society, the subtleties and paradoxes of leadership, humanity's pursuit of happiness, the potential of the human race, possible solutions to environmental challenges, what is needed for an improved future for our planet, and so forth.

In these particular conversations you are about to read, we talk much more directly about what one could call the science or understanding of spirituality, or Self-Realization. I was especially surprised by how curious and open Russell was to really understand my point of view without interrupting that process due to skepticism, which could have stopped the flow of our dialogue mid-way. Our conversations went to depths I had not expected. Russell genuinely attempted to get to the bottom of my experience on this broad topic. He paused me only when he needed to understand something better in order to continue to follow my narrative with some measure of accuracy and confidence; never to ridicule or outright dismiss something I proposed.

I was surprised by how deeply Russell was willing and able to investigate certain topics that modern or mainstream scientists or intellectuals would never even touch upon. In these dialogues, I would say he managed to put his skepticism bandwidth aside almost altogether, and instead, stepped into the joyful spirit of what is the best and fastest student that life has ever known: the curious child. This attitude or bandwidth, combined with his intellectual capability, allowed for truly in-depth explorations between what one could loosely categorize as a spiritual teacher or philosopher, and an atheist, neurologist and skeptic.

I hope you enjoy this interaction. A joyful meeting of such different worlds is not something that happens every day —at least not in the form of a harmonious, in-depth dialogue. Admittedly, I do most of the talking in these conversations, and they ended up being more like interviews than dialogues.

It is my wish that this may be an exciting and refining read for those already deep into these understandings; an eye-opener and mind-expander for those just starting out on their spiritual journey; and potentially inspiring for some of you to share with the open-minded or curious skeptics many of you call your family and friends.

Many blessings,

Bentinho

CREATION, AWARENESS & INFINITE REALITY

Bentinho: Alright! Let's get it on, Russell!

Russell: Ah ha!

Bentinho: Let's prove some things.

Russell: Let's play some truth.

Bentinho: Alright. So [pointing at the book Descartes, which Russell was just reading], "I think therefore I am." Do you agree with that?

Russell: Yeah. I figure he's got one more half step with him. He thinks that there is what is called a *substance duality*. He thinks the mind is a totally separate substance than the body. So the mind is immaterial, spiritual. That's what he's most sure about.

Bentinho: Cool! How about you?

Russell: I like it.

Bentinho: I think that's progress! [Here Bentinho is sort of jokingly referring to past dialogues he has had with Russell that left him with the impression that Russell does not particularly adhere to the concept of an immaterial reality being consciousness, mind or spirit.]

Russell: I can't prove that you exist or that my body exists, but I like his thinking. And since I am thinking, there is some thinking processing within me that exists. But I cannot 100% get to anything *material*. First of all, I believe that the mind is based on neuroscience stuff.

Bentinho: So, matter produces the immaterial experience of consciousness?

Russell: I think matter produces consciousness.

Bentinho: In the same breath, I hear you saying that you can't prove there is any materiality, but you can prove that *you are*.

Russell: Yes.

Bentinho: Then you're saying that you believe—meaning you have an assumption which you can't prove—that matter produces the experience that you are.

Russell: Right.

Bentinho: Are you more sure about the thing you are *not* assuming, or are you more sure about the thing you *are* assuming? Meaning, are you more sure about matter producing *I am*, or are you more sure about *I think therefore I am*, and that matter cannot be proven?

Russell: I'm more sure about the *I am* part. Absolutely. And I live my life and I completely believe that it's caused by material events going on in my body. The brain is a funny thing.

Bentinho: So, you're saying that you're pretty sure about *I think therefore I am*, and you're less sure about your belief that it's the brain or matter that produces the experience of *I think therefore I am*. You believe that, without the matter part, there would not be that capacity.

Russell: Right.

Bentinho: So, you're not completely sure about materiality producing *I am* or consciousness, but you are sure about *I am*.

Russell: I would say I'm somewhere between 100% and 99.9999% sure that matter produces consciousness.

Bentinho: Ha! That's all we need; just give me that .0001%! [Laughter]

Russell: You got it! I could be in the matrix [referring to the movie, *The Matrix*] or in a video game or whatever. So, how do you get to 100%? I'm not 100% sure about anything material.

Bentinho: I'm not either. In fact, I would say that I'm 99.9999% sure of the opposite of what you're saying.

Russell: Wow.

Bentinho: Ironically, this happened through my experience of *I am* deepening and becoming more direct, with fewer and fewer thoughts and assumptions. It's like pulling on the end of a little thread sticking out of your sweater. You just keep pulling and pulling, and eventually, the whole sweater comes apart, revealing it to be nothing but that one thread. It's kind of like that with the direct experience of *I am*.

Russell: Descartes talks about how material things have *extension*—that's what makes them material. Anything material is in 3D space; it is three-dimensional, basically. The mind, on the other hand, is not extensible; you can't tear it apart or whatever. The problem with this is that the mind *is* sort of extensible. You can have a stroke and lose your ability to speak or you can have a metabolic problem and lose your short-term memory. Or you can be part of a split-brain experiment and have kind of like two brains—two worlds even.

Bentinho: For me, what resolves this type of question is that what you are describing is the *content* of the mind; not the mind itself. So, perhaps a worthwhile distinction to consider is: Is the content of perception the perceiver itself?

Russell: You're talking about the essence of the mind?

Bentinho: Even though it's not a physical container, you could say the mind is sort of a container of contents or appearances. You could describe it as essence and form. I would say that the *contents* of consciousness do not define *consciousness*. So, whatever happens to the contents of consciousness isn't actually happening to consciousness; it's happening to the contents of consciousness only. It's appearing to consciousness, but not affecting its essence.

Let's take, for example, a person with bipolar disorder or someone who, after a stroke, can't speak or think as they could before. This does not impair the mind essence itself, it just impairs their ability to express in a certain way. It affects the contents of the mind. Instead of *mind* we could say *consciousness*.

Russell: Can you define mind or consciousness?

Bentinho: Yes. It is sentience. Awake, aware, alive is-ness. It *is*, as opposed to anything else.

Russell: It is? Is that what you said?

Bentinho: Yes.

Russell: What about sedative drugs? They go into the body and affect awareness.

Bentinho: Do they though? Or do they affect the *contents* of awareness?

Russell: I think sedative drugs affect the level of alertness or awareness, for example, when you are drunk-drunk, like Suzie was when she drove her car into a pole a couple of years ago. She doesn't remember any of it, so her awareness was affected.

Bentinho: But if her awareness was affected, shouldn't it still be impaired?

Russell: No, because it was a temporary effect of the alcohol.

Bentinho: She doesn't remember it, but her awareness is unaffected.

Russell: Her awareness now?

Bentinho: Yeah. If you cut off a leg, it's cut off forever. But if you have memory loss or personality loss or whatever, your *I am* is still your *I am*. It is not affected.

Russell: Are you talking permanent or temporary? Temporarily, her awareness was affected. Do you agree with that?

Bentinho: I don't, and I can explain why. The *contents* of her awareness were affected. This is a little hard to prove unless you have direct experience with, for example, being aware of being in deep sleep. Most people are not able to do this because for their whole lives (and arguably longer), they have been focused on *form*. They are always focused on form.

Would you agree that we are virtually always focused on objects, whether these are physical objects, objects of thought, ideas, feelings, conversations, other people, or future dreams or desires? These are what I call *appearances* or *perceptions*. Appearances seem to be objects; they operate as if they are objects. We can't prove that they are actual, independently existing objects, and I don't believe they are, but they operate or act as objects to their observer.

What is an *appearance*? It is literally anything that's registered by your awareness; anything you can be aware of. The emphasis is on awareness being aware of something. Whatever awareness can be aware of is an appearance. It arises, it appears and it dissolves again. Appearances are not permanent. They are always changing; always in flux. No object is permanent, you could say.

Russell: Right. OK.

Bentinho: However, the awareness that recognizes the contents of your life, all of the appearances, is the same now as when you looked in the mirror at the age of three. This awareness was not impaired when Suzie got drunk and had memory loss. What was impaired was her conscious sense of who she is. But that constructed sense of herself as a conscious person is not actually the awareness itself; it's the contents of awareness—images, ideas, functions, etc.

What I'm saying here is that there is an awareness of memory loss; the object or appearance in this case was memory loss. This is a little hard to prove unless you have direct experience with standing beyond such contents, but there is an awareness of memory loss, just as there is an awareness of having no mind or no conscious thoughts or no particular objects in deep sleep. This can be practiced by withdrawing attention from objects. Putting our attention on objects is a habit that's hard to break; it takes a lot of practice and perseverance. But it is possible and I have experienced it myself.

Russell: What have you experienced?

Bentinho: Awareness in deep sleep. *I am* without thoughts or waking consciousness; knowing deep sleep. Knowing no conscious experience, but being sentient and aware of that sentience.

Russell: You remembered it, so it was stored in memory as well.

Bentinho: Uhmm... not really. I have experienced it, so it was confirmed to me, and it's locked-in at a really deep level. But I don't have a memory of it based on images or anything, at least not in the conventional sense of memory, because memory was not there. It's a different state of awareness, you could say. It's a state of awareness or being with no contents. What if this substratum of being is always here, but is so subtle and formless that we have not trained ourselves to be able to recognize it consciously?

We're not aware of this awareness because we have become so absorbed in our object-based sense of who we are. When we wake up in the morning it's like, "Oh yeah, I'm back, because I feel myself in relationship to thoughts, the objects in my room, space-time appearance, and so forth." And when we go to sleep, it's like, "Oh, I'm gone, because I don't see anything I can relate to with a sense of me." Well, we're not actually saying "I'm gone," because we're not there to say such things when we enter deep

Spirit

sleep. We just sort of feel like we're gone in re
because we were not conscious of subject and ob

There are many ways to say all this, but we could say that
there is consciousness and then there is awareness, which
is beyond consciousness. *Awareness* would be the container or essence of mind; *consciousness* would be the personal mind that experiences itself as the subject relating
to the objects of its dynamic focus. But consciousness is
not always aware of the pure existence, or awareness,
"underneath" itself. If you learn to become aware of that
awareness, that deeper, formless *I am* or beingness, then
you can stay with it and more or less become absorbed in
it by keeping your attention on that subtle, formless realization. You can lock your attention onto it, and then, no
matter what happens inside of consciousness, no matter
what happens experientially, your sense of existence can
stay intact.

Russell: OK, so let me kind of rephrase this in my own
words. People have awareness. We are bombarded with
information through all of our senses all the time. Awareness is a focus on part, or a few parts, of that. I can be
aware that you're sitting here, that there is smoke from
your cigar, that there are sounds happening, and so on. I
am aware of these things. Now, if I am aware that I am
aware of these things, then that's *self awareness*.

Bentinho: Awesome!

Russell: What you're calling *consciousness* might be what
I am calling *awareness*. Maybe. And what you're calling
awareness might be what I am calling *self awareness*. Does

27

that sound right?

Bentinho: Yes. But what I'm saying is that awareness is always here, whether you are aware of it or not. That's the only distinction I would make.

Russell: Right. And I would say that I would still be aware of stuff, even if I didn't have self awareness at that time. I'm good with that, I think.

Bentinho: OK.

Russell: But also, if I was drunk right now, my awareness would be decreased. I would be less aware of my sensory data and my thoughts. I would be less aware of my awareness. My awareness and my self awareness would be decreased.

Bentinho: I would say your *sense* of awareness and your *sense* of self awareness would be decreased, but that which *knows* that your sense of awareness is decreased is aware no matter what. It's formless and indestructible. It's immaterial yet real.

Russell: You're saying that there is something there that's core, that's not affected by drunkenness.

Bentinho: Beautiful! I couldn't have put it better myself.

Russell: So, how would you test that? You were talking about the three-year-old self that hasn't changed.

Bentinho: Yes. Can you get a sense of that—a sense of

when you looked in the mirror at the age of three? Can you recapture that and focus on your self awareness during that moment, even if in that moment itself you were not aware of that awareness?

You can actually go back into any memory and observe how there was a background, or core, of awareness that was witnessing the whole thing, even though you weren't conscious of it at the time (so it's not in your immediately stored memory of that moment). This witnessing happened regardless of what you thought or were conscious of. This is also where the conscious mind, the subconscious mind and the unconscious mind are transcended, if you will—they are transcended by this background awareness, which is aware of what you are conscious of and what you are not conscious of.

So, I'm saying that there is a deeper awareness. Your *conscious mind* is that which is currently aware of subject-object relationships. It's mostly aware of objects actually, but that infers the subject. The *subconscious mind* includes all the content that you have experienced, although you were not necessarily consciously aware of the subject-object relationships in that moment.

All of these contents or appearances, whether they are conscious or subconscious to us, are witnessed by something deeper—by a deeper awareness that doesn't change; by a deeper awareness that itself is free of objects, meaning it exists with or without object perception. And this is where the conscious mind, as you know it, lacks an ability to test it. The conscious mind depends on objects, and that's where the basic sense of *ego* comes from. When awareness meets an object, it creates sort of an additional assumption—the assumption of a *relative identity*.

Imagine a formless, space-like void that's indestructible, sentient, awake, alive and aware, but has no form. You could almost say it has no self awareness. It just is.

Russell: So wait... A void? A vacuum? Nothing?

Bentinho: Yes. Just imagine it.

Russell: OK, go ahead.

Bentinho: The point of the analogy is that there is no object. Imagine infinite space with no stars or planets. Suddenly, you introduce a toy; let's say a water pistol. Or it could be a body even. But let's say...

Russell: An object.

Bentinho: Yeah, an object. A water pistol.

Russell: With water in it.

Bentinho: Maybe with Coca-Cola in it.

Russell: With Coca-Cola in it. OK.

Bentinho: Ah! Now there is *something*. Something is created. First there is this space, which is like the pure subject with no reference points. It's like space, but it's not actually space.

Russell: Wait... where am I in relation to this infinite space?

Bentinho: You are it.

Russell: I am it?

Bentinho: Yes.

Russell: OK. But there is nothing in it at first.

Bentinho: Correct. There is nothing in it at all; there is just Infinity.

Russell: But I am in it.

Bentinho: You are it.

Russell: But I am nothing...

Bentinho: You are it.

Russell: I am it. So, I am the whole thing.

Bentinho: Yeah. You are Infinity. You are the One, the one original Infinite before anything was ever created. Before the Big Bang. No form, no body, no neuroscience, no anything. No Coca-Cola pistol.

You have no self awareness in the typical sense because there is nothing to reference; it's just infinite and formless. If you now introduce an object, let's say a water pistol... well, let's say a body, and now a planet. OK, so a planet appears, and on that planet a body appears. Now there are dimensions.

Russell: A human body?

Bentinho: Yeah, a human body. Let's say Russell's body; your body.

Russell: My body? My dead body?

Bentinho: Hahaha... [Bentinho actually thought Russell said "My dad body," a modern-day reference to "dad jokes" or "dad jeans."]

Russell: So, there is an infinite void which somehow is me, and we are going to throw a planet in there. And my body. My dead body.

Bentinho: Yeah, with the focal point being the body. Suddenly the body gets really emphasized. Voop! It just appears. This void, which is aware, becomes aware of something for the first time. First there is an appearance, and that appearance generates a relationship between that aware formless existence and the object. Instantly, a subject-object relationship appears.

Russell: So as the original void, the infinite void, I have the capacity for awareness, but I don't have it if there is nothing else there to...

Bentinho: You are *aware*, but you have the *capacity* for self awareness. Before there is self awareness there is awareness. It's just not aware of itself. It has no actualized knowledge of itself because there is nothing other than itself. It's "just" aware Infinity.

Russell: So that's before the planet is added. How does "nothing" have awareness?

Bentinho: Let's try it the other way around. How could it not be so? If we have awareness as humans, it must be borrowed. Well, that's my supposition. Any type of power comes from a source, wouldn't you agree? Whether it's electricity or anything we could observe physically?

Russell: Yeah, I agree with that.

Bentinho: So, the power to know, which we possess, must be derived from something. It must be borrowed.

Russell: "Borrowed" is tough.

Bentinho: OK, it's just a word. What would you prefer?

Russell: Well, it comes from something...

Bentinho: Something precedes it. Does that make sense?

Russell: Yeah.

Bentinho: There is some source prior to the power to know, prior to the experience of sentience. To me, the fact that there is the power to know is evidence of the capacity for knowing. It's evidence that there is a deeper source, an intelligence and an awareness as sentience, that is able to...

Russell: It's not material-based.

Bentinho: No, it's not material-based.

Russell: Make some blank space here; I'm using every square inch of this paper. [Russell draws a diagram.] Alright, so over here you've got memory, symbol manipulation, and you've got focus. You've got a circuit here. Part of the brain mainly has short-term memory. Part of the brain can manipulate symbols—which for most people is the language function, although it doesn't have to be. And there is an ability to focus attention. You've got impulses—neurons going back and forth. You've got connections going.

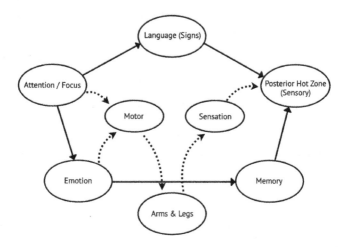

How could that system not have awareness? How could it not have self awareness? Maybe I'm not conveying it well, but I think consciousness comes from this basic system.

Bentinho: I agree that the consciousness you are referring to is a tertiary sense of consciousness that is the product of these types of elements (or components or appearances or objects). It's like you put sunlight and water together and the third effect you get is a rainbow, which is illusory in a sense. I mean, it's real as an *experience*, but it's derived from other components; the rainbow has no independent existence of its own.

Put A and B together and you get some kind of a C. This is applicable in many ways. Like, put a subject and an object together and the relationship between them generates its own appearance; it's own sense. Does that make sense?

Russell: Yeah.

Bentinho: Cool. So, I think what you are referring to as *consciousness*, in this sense, is that rainbow effect; the tertiary product of other components of other appearances. And I'm saying that this rainbow-effect-like consciousness (or *ego-consciousness*) is still an appearance, as it includes components like memory, symbol manipulation and focus.

Russell: Yep.

Bentinho: But these things could not appear without a prior power. Nor could the third effect appear without a prior power. I'm saying there is something in you that sees all that and knows all that. *There is an awareness of your produced sense of consciousness.*

Russell: I guess where we differ is that I think this could be built materially. And I think AI [artificial intelligence] will eventually get to it.

Bentinho: Yeah, I agree [regarding AI]; very probably it will. But still, for me, in order for anything to even be known, there must be a prior source of intelligence—a sentience, a knowingness, a creator or awareness of some capacity. An intelligent, awake, alive reality that is prior to anything else being known.

Russell: Can you say that again?

Bentinho: Sure. I'll make it a blanket statement: Before anything—literally anything—can appear, there must be *something to which it appears*. That's a slightly different way of saying it. There must be a power that manifests experience.

Russell: OK. So let's go back. I believe in the Big Bang, so I think there was some unintentional event...

Bentinho: I would ask you to hold off on the "unintentional" part, just for a moment. I think there was a Big Bang as well, but the intentional or unintentional part—let's park that for a minute.

Russell: OK. We will leave that out; that's fine. The Big Bang created matter; it somehow converted energy into matter. So now we have *things*.

Bentinho: Yes. But I would question you on the origination point of the Big Bang. Where did the Big Bang come from? Because if you would say the Big Bang came from nothing, not as in a reality of formless nothingness, but as in actually nothing, as in non-existence, and that the Big Bang was the first thing to exist... To me it feels very counterintuitive to imagine that out of nothing, out of non-existence, the Big Bang appears and suddenly there is existence. That seems very weird; very odd.

Russell: Yeah, I agree.

Bentinho: Even if I didn't have the direct experience and confirmations that I've had through my meditations and through my journey of retracing consciousness back to its source, I would immediately intuitively ask, "Well, what preceded that? What did it come from? Did it literally come from nothing—just suddenly there was a Big Bang?" That makes no sense.

Russell: Right. I agree. But if your solution to that is that there was some consciousness or some awareness that created the Big Bang, that doesn't solve...

Bentinho: Let's say some *reality*, rather than some *consciousness*.

Russell: OK. But if it's an organized reality, then that just kicks the can further down the road; it doesn't solve anything.

Bentinho: What do you mean by "organized" reality? Intelligent? Is that what you mean—an intelligent reality?

Russell: Well, I assume there is some organization necessary to create something; to create the Big Bang.

Bentinho: I'm a little unclear on what you mean by *organization* because I am then picturing elements, components, duality, appearances, matter—things to be organized. That's already a complex of concepts. If the Big Bang was first; if it was the origin of all organization, of all matter, of all experience, of all appearance, of all perception, of all light, and so on, then hypothetically, before the Big Bang none of that was here. There was no ability to have an organization of components because there were no components. The Big Bang is the origin of perceptible components.

Russell: Right.

Bentinho: So then, what's before that? I wouldn't call it *organizational*. I would call it *reality*.

Russell: What reality are you talking about?

Bentinho: Absolute Reality.

Russell: What is that?

Bentinho: It's hard to describe, but based on my studies, contemplations and mostly direct experiences, I would call it the one original, infinite, formless, indescribable…

Russell: Sounds like Descartes…

Bentinho: Good! He must have had his shit together.

Russell: So it's infinite, and what other words would you use to describe it?

Bentinho: The first word would be *unity*, because infinity must be a unity, by definition. You can't have two infinities, because the first must end and somewhere the other must begin, which means it's not infinite. So, infinity by it's very definition, must be a unity. Does that make sense?

Russell: Sure.

Bentinho: Infinity is very difficult—I would say impossible—for us to comprehend from any level of consciousness that bases its sense of self and its ability to comprehend things on its former relationship to, or awareness of, objects, concepts, components, appearances etc. Because infinity is none of these things; it is not an object. So with this current state of consciousness, or mind, we can think of it, we can imagine it...

Russell: Well, we can't really imagine infinity. Maybe you can, but for most of us, it's a non-negative. We can think of big finite things and try to assume there is no limit to them, but...

Bentinho: Well, I can't imagine it either, but I can contact the direct experience of it that I have had. It is indescribable to the mind, to the consciousness that is subject-object based. But it's the reality that precedes any manifestation...

Russell: How do you know that it goes back to before the

Big Bang?

Bentinho: Because I have experienced it. I have experienced the end of all of Creation, and therefore what was before the Creation began, as well. Because to the Infinite Timelessness, beginnings and endings lose their meaning. It is a timeless source. The entire Creation, which seemingly contains billions of years of evolution, is nothing but the blink of an eye compared to this infinity.

Russell: Were you outside of time?

Bentinho: Absolutely. There is no time. It's absolutely timeless. *Timeless* is another word for it because time needs objects.

Russell: Other than your direct experience, I am trying to get to the logic of it.

Bentinho: Yes, me too. Haha.

Russell: Just for now, I am going to doubt your direct experience, as Descartes might do.

Bentinho: Great.

Russell: So, to get outside of time…

Bentinho: You know what the beauty of it is? Through practices like imagining timelessness, you can kind of stop the faculty of your mind. When you imagine timelessness deeply and with great one-pointedness for an extended period of time, the mind stops. It just kind of ends. If you really imagine timelessness or infinity for long enough and with enough focus, the mind itself—the subject-object relationship-based consciousness, the rainbow effect—disappears for a moment. Much like it seems to do in deep sleep or unconsciousness.

And what you may discover in that moment, if you go totally into it and maintain it for long enough, is that *you* still exist. But not as a body, not as a mind, and in the final state, not even as a consciousness. You still exist, but as the Infinite Reality. You realize directly, without the intellect as a mediator to understanding, that you exist before Creation (and therefore also after Creation supposedly ends), and that everything else is a subset of that; an illusion stepped down from the original infinite state. A distortion of the original infinity. An appearance.

To make it experimentally confirmable or testable for yourself, first recognize that you are the witness of every event, every object, every appearance and every perception you have ever experienced. Even as all of that passes —time, space, objects, sense perceptions—there is some primordial quality, if you will, of being or is-ing there. Something that seems to be aware and has the power of intelligence or sentience; something that *is*, throughout all of it. That's kind of the bridge to the Infinite Reality.

Russell: What about causality? What do you do with that?

Bentinho: As in?

Russell: I throw a rock towards the pond and then I hear it hit the pond. Is that an illusion of time?

Bentinho: Yes, as an experience.

Russell: OK. How does time fit in with the universality of presence? How is there a causality to everything that has happened? Because if the past and the future are all existing now—I think that's kind of what you experienced—how do you explain what I would call *time*, or the apparent experience of time? Of this time now and of the past?

Bentinho: I would say it is simply an illusion. When you are dreaming at night, you have many experiences and perceptions. Then, when you wake up, you realize that actually, there were no objects. "I seemed to have had a body. I could hear people call my name, but I didn't actually have any real, material ears. I could see people walking around, but I didn't actually have any eyes. I could feel things touching my body, but I didn't actually have a body."

So the experience of the dream seemed real, but in reality, it had no substance, other than being an illusion of consciousness perceiving its self-generated content. Perception of content, including time, is somewhat real as an *experience*, but it's not real as a *reality*. It doesn't have a nature independent from consciousness. And it's not permanent or changeless, which an absolute reality must be, or it would not deserve that name.

Russell: In your regular life, which time do you use more often?

Bentinho: I suppose that's where the personal challenge, if you want to call it that, comes in. How to live life after you have experienced this. What do you prioritize? Because the dream appears—at least to a certain portion of my sense of being; not to all of it. How relevant is it? Causality, body, law, government, other-selves, time, the years passing by—all of that still appears, and I'm simultaneously very aware of it being an illusion. So then what do you prioritize? What can you still believe in or stand for? It becomes sort of a meta-personal challenge at that point. A living, breathing, dream-like paradox. Especially when your own ideas or points of view are all transmuted into emptiness or non-locality or non-reality.

I can't say I have fully resolved every portion of this living, multi-dimensional paradox, but I have transcended many such paradoxes and meta-challenges, and have come to terms with the ones that seem to remain in some capacity. I have accepted it and have begun to enjoy it. To love it. Deeply. And in that deep acceptance also lies a transcendence. So even the paradoxes that I do not yet have a final answer for, so to speak, or would not be able to fully explain with 100% confidence to another, I appreciate as being part of the one infinite mystery. It begets a sense of profound love for all of Creation and all the beings that seem to occupy it.

I experience it all as a simultaneity at this point. There is a simultaneity of the dream happening, of the realization that it's an illusion, of the seeming substratum-appearance of awareness or *I am*, and of this changeless and absolute Infinity. I can make this more pronounced, or I can make the dream more real or pronounced, depending on what I guide my consciousness to. It can kind of slip in either direction on the illusion-reality and diversity-uni-

43

ty spectrums.

Russell: If the dream is causing you anxiety, do you try to use the other, the absolute... what do you call it? Absolute time?

Bentinho: We could call it *the Absolute.*

Russell: So then, do you use that perspective to try to...

Bentinho: That's one way, and I have used that in times of more intense suffering or confusion, yeah. But at the same time, I have also become appreciative and embracing of the mechanics and the intelligence behind the structure of the dream, and of the purposefulness of the illusion. Here, we get into a sort of poetic understanding of it perhaps. But I've also come to terms with it as in, "Yes, it is unreal, but it serves a purpose." It is actually based on an intelligence; it has an intent. There is an intention behind the dream appearing.

Russell: And is the purpose just for the illusion of it? Or for other people's perceived happiness?

Bentinho: Do you mean contributing to others' happiness?

Russell: To contribute to other people who are still deluded, or...

Bentinho: Yes. That's the result when someone wakes up and realizes this infinite reality, which also comes with a limitless sort of joy or bliss. It's hard to describe. It is transcendent of body and mind, and even spirit, as in an individual consciousness. At that point, the purpose for that particular entity (if they so choose, from the deepest part of their remaining individuated illusion or free will) becomes to unplug people from the matrix, if you will.

But from a larger view, what is the purpose of the illusion? Billions of years of Creation and evolution and different dimensions; space and planets and revolutions around trillions of suns; an infinite variety of life forms and journeys... There is an intelligence that makes all that tick. Anyone who disputes this is simply stuck in their minds and filled with arrogance or delusion. All of this infinite dreaming—the universe—can't just happen randomly. Well, that's my experience anyway, both intuitively and...

Russell: Then, if it's an illusion, if it has all already happened or it's all happening in the present, we are just sort of suffering through in earthly time what is universally present, what already exists.

Bentinho: Yeah. That's the irony.

Russell: What is the purpose of that? Is it an exercise?

Bentinho: In terms of its purpose in a more relative sense, from the perspective relevant to the human dream in this density or dimension, what I have come to is that it's for learning.

Russell: Ah.

Bentinho: But if you take it deeper, all the way to the edge of the soul or the essence of consciousness itself, the purpose is about awakening completely to the infinite reality. Because if we go back to the example of the void, which is not self aware...

Russell: Right.

Bentinho: It is sentient. It is an alive reality; an intelligent infinite reality. But somehow it births the desire to know itself more and more with each Creation cycle.

Russell: Now me as the void—I thought I was not aware. But I am aware?

Bentinho: You are aware, but you may not be aware that...

Russell: I'm not self aware.

Bentinho: Right. You may not be aware in that sense, or at least not as fully as you could be through learning and awakening from the induced dream, which provides Infinity with contrast or difference between the Absolute Self and its seemingly manifested illusion. Like using a mirror to see your own face.

Russell: In your words, I am *conscious* but not *aware*?

Bentinho: I would say that you are *aware* but not *conscious*. [Laughter] Usually, if I have to make a distinction for teaching purposes, I say that awareness is deeper and prior to consciousness. Awareness is the changeless. Consciousness is the rainbow effect, based on subject-object relationships, that happens or appears inside of the changeless awareness.

Russell: *Consciousness* for you is what I call *self awareness*.

Bentinho: Yes. I see.

Russell: So, the void is aware, but it's not conscious until there is something else to...

Bentinho: This becomes really hard to describe, but I have directly experienced what I believe is the desire that gave birth to the Big Bang. Or to all Big Bangs for that matter. It's not *desire* as we know it, though.

Russell: You have experienced this desire?

Bentinho: Yes. Ironically, it's the desire from infinite Perfection, from infinite Unity, to know itself—even though, in another sense, it already completely and fully knows itself. But paradoxically, there is the desire for actualization of its self awareness, so to speak. Therefore, it generates the illusion of something other than itself, which it can then use as means to express itself in an infinite number of ways.

In the more final stages of evolution, it can also use the illusion as a mirror to see itself in contrast to the manifest. It gets really impossible to describe these experiences in language understandable to the human-based mind. We can only approximate these timeless living truths by means of analogy and contrast. To directly know these types of things for yourself, you will have to go beyond the mind and even beyond the soul. Ultimately, you will even have to go beyond pure beingness-consciousness, or the primal God-soul, if you will. All of this is possible, but requires clarity, profound desire and the resulting practice.

Russell: The desire to know itself suggests that Infinity, this perfect Infinity, was lacking something.

Bentinho: And again, that's where it becomes really hard to talk about because those are very dualistic terms. Even though it's not lacking anything, somehow it desires to express, actualize and gain further knowledge of itself.

Russell: You get to say that?

Bentinho: I'm trying to say it in words that are human, since the conversation we are having is happening inside the human mind.

Russell: OK, let's play with this a little, because I think it's a contradiction.

Bentinho: Let's call it a *paradox*.

Russell: OK, a paradox then. So, we're just gonna live with that, like we live with the Christian holy trinity?

Bentinho: Hahaha! Well, my company is called Trinfinity...

Russell: I know that. In your trinfinity, what are the three things?

Bentinho: The Infinite or Absolute Reality is one. The manifestation of Creation, or the universal presence of all that is, is one. And the individual, the individuated experience, or the mind/body/spirit-based seeker is one. I don't know if you have seen our logo symbol; it's the infinity sign but with three loops. Awareness is the line itself; the bridge between the three components of the infinite. [Bentinho draws the trinfinity sign.]

Russell: You don't have consciousness in the logo?

Bentinho: Awareness produces different states of consciousness; different experiences of consciousness.

Russell: Awareness produces consciousness...

Bentinho: By the way, in my philosophy there is nothing apart from consciousness, so everything is a form of consciousness. To me, this table is a form of consciousness experiencing itself as it is, having a very partial, unique, narrow type of experience of infinity. But like a hologram, it contains all of infinity.

Russell: I want to go back to this idea of desire without lack. So, this perfect Infinity had a desire, and this is something you have sensed.

Bentinho: Let's replace the word *desire* with *possibility*.

Russell: OK.

Bentinho: I sense the possibility from the Infinite to also create an infinite illusion. Because it's infinite, it also has infinite potential. Therefore, everything that it could ever possibly produce must *be*—including things that are not actually real, like this whole world creation. So, rather than a desire, it's almost like an *inevitability* that comes with infinity. It's not exactly like having the desire for an ice cream cone because you feel like you are lacking the sensation of a sugary treat, and you believe it will make you happy or more complete if you have one.

Russell: But still, why change anything? It is infinite and perfect, so why? If there is going to be any change, it's got to be out of boredom or curiosity.

Bentinho: It's not a change though. If anything...

Russell: It's a creation; it creates itself.

Bentinho: You could say it's an *addition*. But from the timeless point of view, the addition was always already the case too. So, it was never created at some point; it's just part and parcel of infinity to also have infinite illusions of creation(s). But the infinite Perfection never becomes imperfect. It only seems that way from the perspective of an individuated or distorted consciousness. Infinity does absolutely no harm or change, nor does it cause any imperfection to itself by this illusion appearing. Suffering or imperfection is a mental creation or imagination.

Russell: OK, but you went back to universal time.

Bentinho: Universal time—what do you mean by that?

Russell: Ever present, ever presence, the universal presence.

Bentinho: I would say that is still a manifestation. That's the energy that is the substratum of all subsequent forms and illusions and perceptions and individuations. Like the concrete foundation of a house or the gold out of which many different forms of jewelry are made.

There is the infinite reality, or the Absolute, which is absolutely formless and has no manifest presence or definable quality of experience. Then, it produces a virtually infinite presence, or field of aware energy, which, to simplify it, you could say is the *first manifestation*. The primordial appearance. Out of this infinite presence-energy, or manifestation, or illusion-substratum, it then begins to organize itself into patterns of light and vibration, and then into the experience or expression of dimensions, time, individuations, etc. Then the organizational play of evolution begins against the backdrop of the presence-energy of Allness (like the gold in the jewelry). Organization can only be the case if there is an intelligence; otherwise you would have no organization. Chaos cannot become intelligent without already innately containing intelligence.

So, there is the timeless infinity and there is the eternal presence. From our point of view as human observers, *eternal* would equal *timeless*, but eternity is not timeless in comparison to that which has no matter, no energy and no presence or consciousness (as we know it). There is still a gap or distinction between the apparent timelessness in pure presence and the true timelessness of the Absolute, since presence of Universal Consciousness is still a creation, and the Absolute is not a creation. So, it is not truly timeless, but eternal within its own illusion, and it produces the entire universal illusion...

Russell: So it's like Creation. Everything happens in the present and everything *is* the present.

Bentinho: Uh-huh.

Russell: This stuff is hard to understand for worldly beings! [Laughter]

So, it wasn't really caused.

Bentinho: Correct. Beautiful! It wasn't really caused; it was an inevitability that is innate to infinity. Infinity is also the infinite potential for everything; therefore everything has to *be*, or rather, has to *appear to be*. And since infinity is also timeless, the appearance of Creations cannot truly be said to be caused in time. An infinite number of Creations exist in a sort of timeless manner.

Russell: OK. This is tough because we are looking for truth, right?

Bentinho: I know...

Russell: If we were just looking for how to get through this life as best we can... well, that could be worth something too.

Bentinho: I agree. That's the benefit of more relative, or stepped-down spirituality. It's more relevant to where humans are in this stage in their evolution. So, let me ask you this perhaps more practical, or more preferential, question: Would you prefer to figure out how to best navigate or move though this life, in order to better endure / enjoy this life, or would you rather experience sort of a timeless liberation that's free from the constraints of this individuated life? Not that you can't have both, but as a curiosity, if you had to choose. To say it another way: Would you want to know how to live well within the matrix, or would you want to be unplugged? [Bentinho is referring to the movie *The Matrix*.]

Russell: Which pill did you have to take to be out of the matrix? Was it the red pill?

Bentinho: Yes, the red pill.

Russell: If I *believed* that we were in the matrix, I would take the red pill for sure.

Bentinho: Are you sure though? Because it would mean having to give up everything you know, in terms of...

Russell: Well, I would have to assess. Neo didn't have to give up everything in the matrix, like all of its pleasures and stuff. So yeah, I would want reality. But if I don't *believe* there is a matrix, then I wouldn't want to spend a lot of time looking for it.

Bentinho: Yep.

Russell: But I agree, my life so far has been the blue pill—the other pill. You know, just making the best out of what I choose to do.

Bentinho: Cool. There is a range of philosophies which state something I would agree with, which is that there is a level of your consciousness that, just to be clear, is not the Absolute, but it is beyond this physical manifestation of the lifetime that you are having here. And this consciousness, in a sense, registers what you are learning and to what degree you are awakening from the matrix. At the time of your death, this is reassessed by that sort of "meta-consciousness" that still belongs to you as an individual. Call it the *soul* if you will. It reassesses what is the best next dream to dream in order to wake up further, based on the intelligence that it's borrowing from its infinite source.

The ultimate goal is complete liberation and realization of the One by itself, through the mirror of its own Creation; through the illusion of an individual soul that's manifesting many different dreams—thousands or hundreds of thousands of dreams—until it realizes itself through that illusion. And the road along the way has the simultaneous purpose of expressing and experiencing all the infinite ways in which the infinite One can express and know itself in relative ways.

Russell: And when it becomes self-realized, it becomes one with…

Bentinho: With itself.

Russell: Or with the Infinite.

Bentinho: Correct. And then there's no more need to experience any manifestation.

Russell: And if it hasn't reached that point, it comes back.

Bentinho: It has to. Because the primal desire to evolve into full realization is still innately present at the root of this entity's beingness.

Russell: It comes back into another body?

Bentinho: Into a body, yes. Into some type of vehicle for relative, subject-object experience.

Russell: Could it be a rock?

Bentinho: It could be a rock, although in my hierarchical understanding of the evolution of a soul within the illusion of time, rockness comes before humanness. So, from that point of view, I am suggesting that your soul has already experienced millions of years of rockness, then plant and microbial life and animal life—simply stated.

Russell: How far backwards can you go?

Bentinho: To the first elements in their most chaotic condition.

Russell: To the rock?

Bentinho: Those were the first types of bodies or vehicles. They were used for the dream to be experienced in a certain way.

Russell: How many levels are there?

Bentinho: I believe there to be seven. This—our human-ness—is the third.

Russell: So you only have to get through seven levels to...

Bentinho: There are seven different... let's call them *dimensions* or *densities* or *types of vehicles*. Each successive level has greater self awareness. We could say that each has a higher density of aliveness, of self consciousness, of self awareness.

Russell: So someone, a soul, could spend a lot of time in one density; you don't always go up and down. Within a density are there upper and lower...

Bentinho: There are sub-densities, like notes within an octave. It's a spectrum with no real dividing lines, though dividing lines can be inferred because there are thresholds where the experience and type of vehicle change distinctly enough to produce a border of sorts between densities, or stages. But it is essentially a gradient, a continuous spectrum. Each density has its main set of lessons or theme of awakening.

Russell: So presumably, I would be at some level.

Bentinho: Late 3rd Density, presumably.

Russell: Haha!

Bentinho: That's the highest sub-density of 3rd Density.

Russell: I think that's a compliment, but I dunno...

Bentinho: Haha, great!

Russell: And so the next level of progress would be...

Bentinho: Early 4th Density.

Russell: And if I'm going down, how many levels before I get to level 2? How many lives?

Bentinho: Well, 2nd Density is one major density distinction away from 3rd, but you would have to regress a lot to get there. Which is practically impossible. Cavemen, or Neanderthals, or at least the image we have of them, could be said to represent the first type of experience of 3rd Density, where they still lived in packs and were quite animalistic and instinctual in their reasoning, self-reflection and behavior.

You have a vehicle in 3rd Density that—due to its more complex or advanced hardwiring or circuitry—is now capable of fully supporting the ability to self reflect and think abstractly, whereas an animal doesn't generally have that capacity. At least not nearly to the same degree. And some not at all. The animal body is a vehicle for the 2nd Density experience or lesson.

Russell: So when I die, that's when I make my move, if I am going to make it.

Bentinho: So to speak, yeah.

Russell: For most people it's at death; I think that's what you said.

Bentinho: Yes, as I see it, for the vast majority.

Russell: What about for a rock? When is that term over?

Bentinho: As rockness, when you get smacked repeatedly by the beingness of water, and your terrain is worked upon tirelessly by fire and wind, which are your peers or your *other-selves* in 1st Density, you eventually somehow generate the desire for movement, for growth, for greater self-awareness, and ultimately, for a sense of individuation.

Russell: OK, so with rockness there is some...

Bentinho: Some learning.

Russell: Some awareness.

Bentinho: There is some awareness; it's just not self aware.

Russell: So, there is no consciousness. Ha! We are using each other's terms! [Laughter]

Bentinho: But something that is not aware of itself can absolutely grow in its desire to move. If you watch a caterpillar for example, it's not conscious of becoming a butterfly, or at least it doesn't seem that way to me. But there is something in its *blueprint* that knows what to do. There is a level of intelligence and a desire for growth that precedes the entity's conscious abilities and guides the entity without its conscious knowledge toward its desired growth. This deeper, non-intellectual intelligence operates as a type of blueprint for the incarnation. The manifest portion of that entity doesn't have to be aware of the impetus in order for evolution to occur. The impulse, or desire, precedes the understanding of it.

Russell: So, when you were born, what level were you?

Bentinho: When I was born into this body? Me specifically?

Russell: Yeah.

Bentinho: Any soul that incarnates into planet Earth's currently active density (the world as we see it with our senses) has a body and a mind of the nature of 3rd Density. Even if the soul of an entity, if you will, has already been through and graduated from this density in its own "native" history. The same goes for me: my body and the conscious mind that developed during this lifetime are creatures—or the results—of 3rd Density.

Russell: Are you 7th Density now?

Bentinho: I perceive my baseline, or *native state*, if you will, to be of a late 6th Density nature, with penetrative and ongoing maturing experiences of 7th and 8th Density while incarnate here.

Russell: Did you say 8th? I thought there were only seven levels.

Bentinho: 8th Density equals true Infinity. It is the density of Absoluteness, as I like to refer to it sometimes. It is the end, or "after the end," of Creation. In contrast, 7th density is the density of Allness, Foreverness or the Completed Density—the universal, eternal, seemingly timeless presence energy consciousness where all of Creation again comes together into a single point or essence of knowing itself. But it is not yet the original One before the Big Bang. The One is before the experience of oneness.

Russell: So you've advanced (is that a fair word?) four density levels?

Bentinho: My present understanding is that my baseline was already of a late 6th Density nature when I chose to incarnate here. I did this mainly out of the desire to be of service; to answer a strong, collective, energetic calling that was broadcasting from the consciousness and unconsciousness of this collective. I didn't personally need this 3rd Density experience to become ready for the 4th Density experience/expression/lessons. My soul, if you will, already integrated those lessons a long time ago.

This type of incarnation is more commonly known as being an *old soul*, or a *wanderer*. And lately, the New Age community has popularized the term *starseed*. If this makes any sense at all, you could consider the soul responsible for this body-mind projection into this dimension of beingness to be of a late 6th Density vibratory nature in its native evolution, and it/I chose to re-experience the 3rd Density environment because it/I sensed there was a strong collective calling for clarity and harmony on this planet. Great suffering generates a powerful calling, especially when billions are either consciously or subconsciously asking for clarity and harmony.

[*Sidenote to the reader from Bentinho:* In this passage, I was simply flowing with the dialogue, without any idea that this would eventually become a book. So, I wish to interject here that it is not my intention to create a perceived difference between myself and others or to put myself on a pedestal; that would be counter-productive to the desire that brought me to incarnate here to begin with. Therefore, I find it important to share here that, as I understand it, there are literally hundreds of millions of *wanderers* incarnate on Earth at this time with a similar intention. I am, in that sense, not special, more holy or even rare for that matter. There are many wandering souls who show up out of love and compassion, and chances are high you are a wandering soul in service to a calling if you have found yourself attracted to this book. The degree to which I have awoken to my nature by penetrating the veil of forgetfulness inherent in 3rd Density consciousness is—though not special—still rare on this planet today. I am trying to help change that through the types of interactions, teachings and projects we're creating through the *Trinfinity* and *Bentinho Massaro* brands.]

Russell: So, you didn't have to incarnate here?

Bentinho: As I understand it, no, I didn't have to. It was voluntary. I didn't incarnate here due to the demand or out of need of the rhythms of unconscious evolution, but rather as a deliberate choice. It was mainly an act of service to my brothers and sisters behind the veil; a choice to answer this collective calling I spoke of. It was an expression of deep love and compassion born naturally out of the knowingness that is so obvious in the 6th Density vibrations of unity—that all other-selves are in essence myself, and the knowingness that I could form myself in such a way as to be of assistance at this timing in this collective.

There are also added "perks" to coming here, for my "own" development, as well as some risks and challenges, but I understand these to be added attributes or side effects that come along with the choice to "wander across densities." The primary motivation is plain and simple: the answering of a calling. This is not unlike people accepting the duty of joining the military or devoting their lives to a truly charitable organization—or even like you answering an urgent phone call from one of your children—except that this is a very elaborate, layered and involved phone call or job. And it's a call that lasts for a lifetime, or multiple lifetimes, and comes with some unique challenges, opportunities and risks.

Russell: So, you were late 6th Density when you came into this world; when Ben took shape.

Bentinho: On a soul level, yes.

Russell: How much can people advance in one human lifetime?

Bentinho: Potentially, though improbably, all the way.

Russell: So, they can go from 3rd to 6th or 7th.

Bentinho: They can go from 3rd to the end of the universe, to the One before Creation.

Russell: From 3rd to 8th.

Bentinho: Yep.

Russell: Is that one of your goals, to get to 8th?

Bentinho: I've penetrated it, so in that sense I've already "gotten there" or opened the gateway to it. I just haven't decided to exclusively "stay there" (to use very human terms) with my entire awareness or beingness.

There is a choice that, once again, is unfortunately very difficult to explain in human or intellectual language. It usually happens at the moment of penetration into the Absolute Reality, depending on the depth and totality of that penetration, though this choice also permeates throughout everyday life as an ongoing choice in the background of one's consciousness... assuming you have penetrated. If you have never penetrated into the Absolute Reality, which is prior to all consciousness and even before or beyond pure beingness, then this choice is not really an active choice. It remains dormant until penetration occurs.

The choice has to do with whether or not you want to maintain a foothold in the matrix of form, regardless of level. There have been examples throughout human history, though very, very few examples. But there have been some, I do believe, and they describe never experiencing the universe again, or being permanently established as the One, even though their body seems to be doing what it is doing.

This is not the same as the more "typical" enlightenment you see present in many teachers these days. What I am describing is beyond that. The rare few examples describe knowing the Infinite at its undistorted original state, before even consciousness-beingness-bliss. They don't experience a body or a mind or a universe, they don't experience others, nor do they experience beingness as themselves... yet they are still talking. In our world, in our perception, they are talking. This is a bit like watching a famous actor being projected on the screen of a movie theater after he is already dead. Except in this case, the "deceased" actor is fully awake, in and as the one original Reality.

Russell: So, you can be 8th Density and still be engaged and in the matrix.

Bentinho: Apparently. I wouldn't say it's "you" that's engaged in the matrix though; it is the shadow, the trail, or the remnants of that beingness' expression in form that remains for others to perceive. I already experience this myself to a great extent—that I am not the one speaking and walking and talking and creating what it creates. My own incarnate self appears and feels to me like an illusion that does not contain me.

Russell: Is total dissolution your goal?

Bentinho: Total dissolution would equate to late 7th Density; where the individual has merged completely with the Allness or God Consciousness. 8th Density would be better described as complete or absolute transcendence. It is the transcendence even of the experience—or illusion —of dissolution. In the Absolute one also realizes that there is no dissolution; that dissolution, or the loss of self, is also an illusion or trance state of sorts. But yes, such transcendence is my main underlying desire for myself. My more time-based and prevalent desire at this moment is still the completion of my purpose and duty here—to fulfill the reason I chose this incarnation to begin with.

Does the soldier want to go back home to see his family? Sure, but what he wants more is to complete the mission he and his comrades signed up for. The desire to go home and see his family again is ever in the background of his being, yet he maintains an alertness for his current mission and its required tasks. You could say the desire to go home is the desire he has for himself, whereas the desire to fulfill the mission is the desire he carries for other-selves.

So, the meta-personal challenge for me has been to honor the impetus that brought me here to this density of the illusion—to use my relative time here as a springboard for my own soul's development beyond its native point— while also helping as many (apparent) other entities as possible awaken to their potential, both in this life and beyond. Simply by continuing to allow my intuition, clarity and resonance to guide the flow of my actions.

Russell: Well, good luck with me! [Laughter]

Bentinho: It's working...

Russell: Well, you got me thinking, and you've motivated me; I will give you that. Yeah, I will give you that.

Bentinho: More often than not, service is *energetic* too. It's inspiration that can't quite be grokked by the thinking mind. It's like planting the seeds, so to speak, and then the seeds will grow. I'm not responsible for the growth of the seeds, but I can plant them, or at least offer them to someone to plant them for themselves, through my presence, vibration, radiance, and also in some cases, through my words or direct teachings. We all do this in a sense just by being ourselves and influencing others. I'm just more conscious of where that desire comes from, and the ways in which I can do it tactfully and non-intrusively. One of the primary laws of this universe is free will, and it becomes more and more important to uphold as you ascend the ladder of consciousness.

Russell: Can you say more about that?

Bentinho: To honor free will becomes more and more important to an entity as it ascends up the densities of self-realization.

Russell: That's a good topic you are bringing up. So, everything is universal presence. The future has happened, or is happening, and the past is happening.

Bentinho: Yeah, it's all happening simultaneously.

Russell: Simultaneously. It seems to me that this argues against free will, because free will assumes that I can change the future; that I have choice. But if it's all happening right now, it's already set.

Bentinho: That is a limited point of view. [Laughter]

Russell: Well, I'm trying to figure out this universal presence. It seems to me that, if logically followed, that conclusion doesn't follow from our earthly time. But it does seem to follow from a universal presence. So how do you reconcile this?

Bentinho: Let's use the analogy of a film strip. You go to watch a movie. If you deconstruct the film strip, you can see that all the images, from the first few scenes of the movie to the last scene, already exist. Your consciousness is choosing to play these particular frames, these potential creations, in a particular order to give you a unique experience of time and events.

Russell: Yes, that's the earthly time.

Bentinho: Correct. How you *respond* to the scenes in the film, what you learn from it, how you choose to relate to it as a consciousness, as a being, and how it alters your relationship to and understanding of yourself—that is the free will. It's not about whether the pictures you see are new or already existent.

Russell: That is all happening in the present too, universally. So for God, or for this universal time, this universal intelligence, or Oneness...

Bentinho: I would argue and say that *the way you relate* to what already timelessly exists is what is fresh. That's what's new; that's what's cutting edge. And it is the whole reason for this entire illusion; this mysterious and infinite adventure. Even to the Creator and its Allness, or Creation, your choices and realizations have never happened before in exactly the way they occur to your filter of free will.

Russell: Say that again...

Bentinho: The sentience is relating to what appears to be insentient—the events of your life. The events don't have an independent existence apart from the sentient one. They don't exist apart from the observer, or consciousness, but they *seem* to. Every potential experience, every potential perception or object already exists, but how you choose to relate to these perceptions and objects, and how you choose to navigate through the infinite number of frames that are already laid out in a timeless universe— that path or trajectory is what is cutting-edge. That's what is fresh and unique, and it's the result of the primordial principle of free will.

All images or creations that could ever possibly exist, already exist because there is no time. However, on this timeless canvas of infinite structures or configurations of atoms, the free agency of the intelligence of the Creator in the form of individuations is unleashed; it is given free will. That's the expansion of the One knowing itself, and the main reason for this grand illusion, as I see it. In that sense, you are crucial to the expansion of the One's knowledge, awareness and expression of itself.

Russell: So, my soul goes through earthly time, my consciousness goes through earthly time, but everything else, like my material body, goes through universal time.

Bentinho: No, your body is part of the image that already exists. But how you *relate* to your body and its apparent environment—that is your free will. Your body is part of each frame of the movie, just as Tom Cruise's body is inseparable from his environment and the bullets he's dodging. The way you, as a consciousness, relate to this movie is what's fresh and free.

Russell: OK, you have a film strip, and you have this universal time that's seeing everything at once. It's seeing all these stills at... what rate is it?

Bentinho: 24 frames per second is the standard for most movies.

Russell: Right. So, this Oneness has to try to figure out what order these frames are in, because it sees them all at once.

Bentinho: Yes. So, it gives birth to *agents*, or individuations of the Oneness. These individuations are given the experience of free will on behalf of the Oneness. It's like employees in an organization. If you are the CEO of a company, you have to rely on the free will of your employees in order to expand your business and to fulfill the intention for which you created the company. It's like, "Hey, let's explore this portion of our mission, but let's do it through you. You manage it." It's kind of like that, although that's a very simplistic explanation of the reality of it.

Russell: So, this Oneness... I guess that's why people use the word *God*; it's almost easier to think of it that way. But this universal Oneness...

Bentinho: You can call it God.

Russell: OK. This God knows what's happening. It already knows what will happen a minute from now or an hour from now.

Bentinho: It knows what happens structurally because it is already happening.

Russell: It doesn't know what I'm thinking a minute from now?

Bentinho: How you respond to that thought is due to your free will.

Russell: It doesn't know how I will respond?

Bentinho: No.

Russell: Wow!

Bentinho: That's my current hypothesis, anyhow. Now if it wanted to, it could read the *probabilities* of how you are going to respond, based on the context of...

Russell: Probabilities! Now you're in *my* world!

Bentinho: Nice! And yes, ultimately free will is an illusion. But it's only an illusion in the final state—in the state of the Absolute reality prior to the creation of God consciousness. In the Absolute reality there is no time and no Creation, so there is no free will, as such. At least not in any way that we can relate to from this plane. There is only the One itself. Perfect, one, and infinite. No perception of anything but itself. So, you could say free will lies in abeyance until potentially re-activated to begin a new cycle of a Creation.

Free will was part and parcel of the first manifestation, and then that free will, or intelligence, began to generate this universe. This was before this free will further individuated itself into endless agents of consciousness. You could say this universe is the product of a single free will, which you could call God. But there are an infinite number of free will "extensions" of this that create other universes. Since all of these extensions are derived from the one original Infinity, you could think of them as the same free will in different installments, or Creations. We could think of each Creation as an incarnation of the One. Each such incarnation we could call God—the active, executive principle of the one, infinite, absolute Reality.

So ultimately, even God is an illusion, and in that sense, free will is too, because free will belongs to God. But it is the first and primordial illusion. Everything else perceivable follows this initial manifestation or "distortion" of the One.

Russell: So you're saying that people *do* have free will and they *don't* have free will. That's what I'm hearing.

Bentinho: Yes. For all intents and purposes, as long as an

71

entity experiences itself as a beingness, it has the experience of free will; free will is granted. That means that what you choose next is not already set, though there are probabilities based on previous experiences which form biases in the beingness.

Russell: So, I have choice.

Bentinho: Yes, but that choice—not the choice of what you are choosing, but the fact that you even *have* a choice —is also at the same time a fundamental illusion. However, as long as you experience any type of form, creation, world, life, etc., you are under the influence of free will, and it's best to understand or approach it as such.

Russell: So, I go to Ben & Jerry's and I'm trying to decide between vanilla and chocolate ice cream. Do I have free choice as to which one?

Bentinho: According to my findings, yes.

Russell: OK. Let's say I'm going to leave for Ben & Jerry's right now. In 20 minutes when I get there, I will be making this ice cream decision. Does God or this Oneness know which flavor I'm going to pick?

Bentinho: Well, there are infinite versions of you that pick either flavor.

Russell: So now the universe is… there are multiple...

Bentinho: Yeah, you could see it that way. But what you choose to experience is unique to your choices as an individuated expression of God's consciousness. And the more aware you become, the less unconsciousness you have.

Russell: Is there any entity that knows which flavor I'm going to pick in 20 minutes?

Bentinho: Yes, to the extent of probability. And here's why. Entities of a higher density of consciousness can read into the probabilities of your consciousness. Although your consciousness is more complex in nature, it is similar to how you could predict the trajectory of a snail (a 2nd Density being) when it is approaching an obstacle in its path that it is not yet aware of. A higher density entity not currently incarnate as a 3rd Density body-mind, can see how much of you is conscious and how much of you is unconscious. The higher their density, the higher the accuracy of their observations and probability readings. If they read in your unconscious that there is a strong bias towards tea rather than coffee, they can predict with high accuracy that you are going to pick the tea, to use a simplistic example.

Russell: So, they are not 100% accurate; there is some randomness.

Bentinho: I believe so, yes. But rather than randomness, I would say there is mystery, surprise, free will, and endless possibility inherent in consciousness at any given nexus point in one's space-time experience.

Russell: So, even though this universal Oneness, which is outside of time, can theoretically look ahead 20 minutes from now because it's all the same, and can know what I will choose...

Bentinho: Well, it could see all the versions of you that choose different things. But your sense of you, which you keep perpetuating, has free will as to which version is going to experience something. The Oneness sees all the versions, including the one currently active in your individuated sense of consciousness.

Russell: How many universes are we talking about here?

Bentinho: An infinite number of universes.

Russell: OK.

Bentinho: Yeah, it has to be.

Russell: What about this one, this universe...

Bentinho: In the seconds between you saying "this one" and "this universe," billions of different parallel moments or universes have been cycled through your consciousness, unbeknownst to you. Billions of parallel realities per second. Think *Planck time*: "There are more units of Planck time in one second than all the seconds since the Big Bang."

Russell: And this Oneness has to keep track...

Bentinho: That's why, in human, simplistic descriptive terms, you could say it has an "organization" to "keep track." In its original state, it doesn't experience any of this. It only comes into play with the manifestation, which starts with the God consciousness or Allness or Oneness level of the Creation. But before the God consciousness, there is just the one original, infinite void, or rather: Reality.

Russell: What do you mean by "before"?

Bentinho: Before God.

Russell: Before time? In time?

Bentinho: Yes. Before the first manifestation; the first manifestation being consciousness, or God, you could say.

Russell: So, there is a universal time that changes? It's not all present? Is it before... before what?

Bentinho: Before the first manifestation, there is the One. The original Reality.

Russell: So, there is the One original and then there is the One, the Infinite... I'm lost.

Bentinho: Haha. I understand. Well, we can park this for now and continue later because I gotta go. This has been great. Thanks Russell D.!

Russell: I hope you enjoyed it. I loved it.

CONVERSATION 2:

DEEPER INTO INFINITE REALITY

Russell: So, *I think, therefore I am.* Descartes was a thinking spirit or mind. He can show that. But then, how does he get to any other reality? I think your answer is that there isn't a material reality, so you can't get to material things. But Descartes thinks you can. Idealists tend to think that the mind is pretty much all there is.

Bentinho: Idealists?

Russell: Yeah. One of the branches of Idealism states that you can only really know yourself through your thinking self. And some of the Idealists also say there's no external reality.

Bentinho: There's the *experience* of an external reality, but I don't believe there's actually an independent nature to what we perceive.

Russell: So for you, when Descartes proves the existence of a material reality, he is mistaken. He thinks he proves it.

Bentinho: How?

Russell: Well, I don't agree with him. His reasoning is that he has perceptions. He perceives that there are things out there, which we can agree with. And if he has perceptions of things, those perceptions must be caused by something. Like, if I see a tree, I have a perception of that. The perception doesn't have to be caused by a tree, but it has to be caused by *something*. There is a perfect, infinite God, and God being perfect, would not deceive. Therefore, that tree must exist.

Bentinho: There are two main assumptions here that are pretty hard to prove for or against. I do agree that something needs to cause perception, or "source it," I would say. But the source or cause of a perception in no way, shape or form has to exist outside the mind, the consciousness or the perceiver of the perception.

That's his first major assumption, based on what you've said he suggests. When you dream at night, the mind itself causes the perception of a tree in your dream. In the same way, the entirety of the Creation is caused by, through and as the One Creator. This is my understanding, experience and conviction. There is a cause for the tree perception, but its cause does not need to come from outside the observer. That would be a major assumption.

Russell: If the perception is not from outside the observer, then you, I and we are being deceived.

Bentinho: OK, but his definition of *being deceived*, which you could also call *illusion*, supposes there is a negative intent behind it, and that a perfect God would not do that. This is his second major assumption.

Russell: Right.

Bentinho: Based on what you've explained about his views, Descartes kind of humanizes the idea of illusion by calling it *deception*. He brings it down to a human level, and humans have a tendency to deceive each other intentionally for self-gain. A perfect omnipresent God would not do that. I agree with that, because if All That Is, or God, is everything, it has no need to gain from its parts at their expense; it sees all as itself. Hence, *deception* loses its meaning. However, what if there's a purpose behind the deception or illusion—an intelligence, a perfect reason, a benign motivation?

Russell: So, there's sort of a higher reason for that deception.

Bentinho: Yes, a reason based in perfect love. The reason it would be based in love is because nothing exists independently from God, and if nothing exists independently from God, then there is only itself. If we look at the microcosms we have here, for example, animal life, no entity wants to hurt itself. This isn't proof of anything necessarily, but it seems logical and intuitive that, if there is only one thing, by nature it doesn't have the idea of negative intent because all there is itself. Nothing wants to hurt itself or deceive itself intentionally.

So, if oneness is true—and I believe it is, since my direct experience has confirmed this to me beyond my ability to intellectually or otherwise oppose or deny it—then one of the fundamental tenets is that any delusion, deception or perception must have its basis in what we would call *love*.

And love is nothing but the innate recognition of insepa-rability.

Russell: That's kind of a low definition of "love."

Bentinho: A low definition?

Russell: Yeah, it's sort of...

Bentinho: Rudimentary? How dare you, Russell! [Laughter]

Russell: Well, we need to define our terms! Don't take it personally... [Laughter]

Bentinho: What do you mean by "a low definition of love"?

Russell: You said that your definition of love is just sort of existing, or... what did you say?

Bentinho: No. Let's look at what we would call *love* at the very fundamental roots of it. And by this I mean true, unconditional, perfect, divine, Godly love. Not human love, as in, "I have a crush on you because I like your hair and I think you can give me what I feel I lack." This is the humanized version of love, which consists of duality and separation and infatuation and obscured manipulation and all that.

Instead, imagine the most perfect unconditional love, like the love you would have holding your baby in your arms. This human analogy comes closer to real love, perhaps. If you take that to a universal scale, before all this human stuff became part of your awareness and conditioning, then love is the innate recognition of oneness, or insepa- rability. In other words, nothing that can be experienced exists apart from itself, and therefore...

Russell: Recognition.

Bentinho: Recognition, realization, knowingness, an awareness of...

Russell: So, sort of an acceptance, then.

Bentinho: Yes. An inescapable awareness of the fact that, before the human illusion sets in—identifying as a sepa- rate body in a separate world, believing things have an independent nature apart from mind or consciousness or the perceiver or self—all is itself. All is you.

Russell: So, God is love. Therefore, the oneness is love, and therefore, if this love-entity recognizes something as being part of itself, that's like sharing love or...? I'm trying to put it into some kind of human terms.

Bentinho: OK. Imagine all bodies are plugged into a motherboard. The motherboard represents the unified knowingness, or unified field of existence. Let's say this is all one field of consciousness with different... Wait, what's your question exactly? Because I feel I can describe this in so many ways.

Russell: I'm trying to figure out what your definition or understanding is of this one universal love. Because it sounds like it's not a human or common understanding of what it means.

Bentinho: OK. I'm saying that there is no such thing as "human love." It doesn't exist. We can only experience the love *that is*, depending on how transparent we are to the love that is; depending on how much our individuated mind thinks as God thinks or sees as God sees.

Russell: OK. So, God—what is it?

Bentinho: God is a unity of energy that is intelligent—super intelligent, unimaginably intelligent, conscious and sentient. It's a living field, if you want to imagine it that way.

Russell: An energy?

Bentinho: Yes. To clarify, this is not the Absolute Reality. God is the first creation or emanation of that reality. God is like the right-hand person or the executive force of the One Infinite Reality. This is what we will call *God*, the active Creator aspect.

Russell: So, God is separate but...

Bentinho: It's not separate.

Russell: So, it's the same, it's one function...

Bentinho: It's a bit like how a dream is not separate from the mind, but at the same time, the dream does not affect or define the mind itself, necessarily. The mind exists, whether it's dreaming or not dreaming, you could say.

In this analogy, the creative principle that produces the dream when you're sleeping at night could be God. Whereas the mind itself would be the Absolute Reality. But this is just an analogy to show that God does not exist apart from the One Infinite Reality. It's just one potential expression that then gives rise to manifestation and experience.

You could say that God is the *experience generator*. The Absolute does not generate experiences; it remains ever alone and infinite, aware only of itself, if you will, when in its own stateless, conditionless state or condition. It is only as and through God consciousness that the One produces experience, or Creation.

Russell: How about if we work backwards. What's the biggest, grandest and most universal? That's the Oneness? But you've got levels...

Bentinho: You've got levels of distorted perception. Before all perception, there is the original Infinite Reality. It cannot be argued with and it cannot be experienced in the typical sense of the word.

Russell: It's all-knowing, all-powerful, all-infinite...

Bentinho: It's all-infinite.

Russell: And it's conscious?

Bentinho: It has an innate comprehension of itself, but in

my experience, this is mainly because of God's Creation. In contrast to experience, it can know itself as that which is beyond experience. In contrast to form, it can know its formlessness. In contrast to qualities, it can begin to realize its quality-less existence. In contrast to finiteness, it can realize itself as infinite. It has the innate capacity of awareness or comprehension. You could say that first there was Infinity, then Infinity became aware.

Russell: In contrast to form, the formless can know itself.

Bentinho: Yes. At the very end of the maturation of the soul, or simply through an extremely intense longing or desire for the absolute truth, Infinite Reality can know itself. This realization doesn't happen frequently in 3rd Density, at least not on this planet, and unlikely anywhere else either. It is the subtlest of realizations. The highest of the high. The densest of the most dense (*dense* in terms of requiring spiritual mass or focus).

It generally requires great maturation of mind and spirit. By this point, many, many cycles of life and death, of different forms and experiences, of suffering and joy, and of chasing desires have been chosen to be experienced, until one reaches a state of inner ancientness and profound orientation toward the One Truth. Then, one's interest is no longer in exploring this infinite universe of form and variety. Instead, there is a strange desire to transcend one's experience of it; to turn one's gaze completely toward the Creator and its Infinite Reality, and away from the Creation or the illusion of experiencing.

It's like an apple ready to fall off the tree. Or like an old person ready to die because they've seen it all, they've been there, they've suffered enough, they've experienced enough, they've learned enough, they've fulfilled enough of their dreams or they've been disappointed enough. At the end of their life there's a certain tiredness, like, "It's OK. I'm done." Can you imagine that?

Russell: Sort of a giving up?

Bentinho: In a negative sense it could be seen as giving up, but if that giving up is not a premature or temporary reaction to failure—if that entity has deeply fulfilled its sense of why it was here in Creation—then it will feel more like a sense of *completion*, like, "I am done." It comes with great joy and a feeling of utter ancientness; it is not a reaction to pain.

After maturation, the youthful interest in digging into things—studying this and doing that, improving this skill and having that relationship, etc.—has been exhausted through experience. It can be positively experienced or it can be negatively experienced, but it's the same principle of doneness or tiredness or completion. So, it can be a giving up or it can be a sense of completion. A satisfaction, perhaps. A fulfillment in recognizing that one is at the end of one's journey.

Imagine billions of years of exploring all kinds of different life experiences and forms, different illusions, different dreams, dimensions, group-consciousnesses, worlds, lessons, saving planets, destroying planets, fighting wars, preventing wars—what have you. It's like waking up in the morning from a dream, and then you dream the next night, and the next night, and the next night... at some point, through a process of maturation, you're naturally done with all the dreaming. Your task as an agent expressing and learning the lessons of the Infinite One has come to an end. You've explored whatever you could possibly explore that would satisfy your inner craving.

At the end of that threshold, there's a complete turning inwards, which in and of itself, is generally a long journey as well. There's a natural dispassion that grows towards form, and finally even towards all perception itself, because perception itself is no longer interesting; experiencing itself is no longer fascinating. If the heart or essence of an entity is not interested anymore, then what would sustain the subject-object relationship? The perpetuity of it is sustained by desire, interest, need, passion and curiosity. The end of such interest cannot be forced prematurely by a vain idea of wanting to realize The Absolute. It has to be a true maturation, in most cases, or it will simply cause imbalances that need rectifying later on in some lifetime or dimension.

But if need, curiosity and interest are truly and genuinely exhausted by means of much experience and spiritual discrimination, and if the entity or the soul starts to feel complete, then what remains for it to do? It's still apparently here, hovering around in Creation. So, it turns its essence, or beingness, or you could say its attention or consciousness, fully towards the Source of it all, which itself is free of it all.

Thus, the entity begins the final stage of its journey home. The war is over; the interest exhausted. Instead of seeking externally, the entity begins to seek internally, in the deepest sense of the word.

At the end of the lifetime of a star system, when the light and all of its experience and perception collapses in on itself; when it turns toward its center or source, this manifests as what we perceive as a *black hole*. It is an entire sub-Creation ready to be absorbed back into Infinite Reality. The same principle applies to an individual such as yourself.

What question were we addressing?

Russell: Yeah, I don't know! I was just trying to get your framework for...

Bentinho: Oh, I remember. There is the perceiver, or the individuated expression of the One, which you currently identify with as Russell. The name "Russell" is given to this seemingly sentient consciousness that sees through these eyes and uses this vehicle, this body and these senses to interact with a world that is apparently outside of itself. But this world is only perceived as outside from the point of view of the body, not from the point of view of your experiencer, your *I am*.

As part of the canvas of your dream, you experience the perception of the mountain being over there and the body being over here. Because of this, you define there to be distance, differences and separation. But you can't know that for sure. When you turn inward to I am-ness, to be-ingness, to consciousness itself, at the expense of looking at objects, you begin to realize your actual self, instead of being entertained by your non-self, or by appearances. As a result, your perception becomes more transparent, more mature and less distorted.

There is an infinite unity, and nothing, no matter how distorted it is, exists independently or apart from it. It is not possible, because again, Infinity has to be a unity. So there can't be something else that's created out of something else—that implies a duality. There can only be levels of perception rested within this unity.

Russell: So, Infinity encompasses all of that.

Bentinho: Yes. Everything that has ever been experienced, any individuation, any sense of ego, any perception, any seeming object in this illusion—somehow it's all a dream inside the Infinite. It cannot come from anywhere else, per the definition of *infinity*. Otherwise, infinity would be finite and there would be another something that created objects or perceptions. So, it all exists within, or is due to, or is borrowed from the One.

To come back to your question about levels, there are simply levels of distorted perception. The less distorted the perception, the more the individuated mind begins to see as God sees and be as God is, and the less it creates its own ideas and notions from a distorted understanding. That's the whole idea of self-realization, purification or enlightenment—the individual merges back into its unified God-Self, and finally, it quantum-leaps beyond that, into the Absolute Source.

Russell: There is the Oneness and the Infinite... there are

at least two levels. When we get to the human form, there can be distortions and sort of a growth that needs to occur if you're going to experience that. But before taking on the human part, we've got this One that includes everything; it's Infinity. Can we call that *God* if we want?

Bentinho: I would call that the *Infinite*, the *One* or the *Absolute Reality*. I make a distinction between that and God. God is not separate from the Infinite, it is simply an expression or a function that's an active principle, as compared to the original stateless, infinite, indescribable formlessness.

In order to manifest or to produce perception, there must be a creative, intelligent principle—pure consciousness or awareness. There must be the illusion of energy and light and patterns and all that stuff, which is what this consciousness generates and organizes according to its creative intelligence or free will. God appears in the Infinite as the CEO of the organization of a Creation.

Russell: What would we call that universal One, the one before God?

Bentinho: Let's call it the *Absolute Reality*.

Russell: OK, the Absolute Reality. Can the Absolute Reality exist without God?

Bentinho: It does. From its own point of view, it does. It is only from God's point of view that Creation even appears.

Russell: I want to explore this stuff, so that helps.

Bentinho: God is a distortion. It is the first distortion.

Russell: Is it a human distortion?

Bentinho: No.

Russell: If there were no sentient beings, no humans, it would still be a distortion?

Bentinho: Yes. It's a very, very transparent distortion. Or you could say it's the least distorted distortion of the One Infinite Reality. But it is still a twist, or a distortion, of the original One.

Russell: Why?

Bentinho: Why? Because it is *some-thing* now, so it is no longer truly infinite. A thing, which is manifested or produced, cannot be the source, nor can it be infinite.

Russell: You are calling God a *thing*.

Bentinho: Correct. But it's not an object as we know it; it is the perceiver and generator of all that is. It is the creator, the perceiver, and the intelligence that is the substratum of all consequent dreaming. It is the dreamer. It is the huge, *apparently* infinite, universal dreamer. But it is not *truly* infinite; it is only infinite in terms of the scope of its ability to generate an infinite number and variety of illusions. Just like a painting, it can take on infinite shapes and colors, each unique depending on its blend, but it can never not be made of paint.

God's only limitation is that it has to be. It has to be *something*; it has to be itself. A thing cannot *not* be itself. It's the same for God and the Creation—it has to be itself, so it cannot truly be infinite and formless and quality-less anymore. Therefore, it cannot be absolute. If it has a quality, even the quality of consciousness or beingness or universal energy, that is still something. It is still a quality; it is still a *thing*. It "comes from" and is enabled by the Infinite Reality, which cannot be described in any imaginable terms, because imaginable terms are part of the illusion of perception or consciousness.

Russell: I think you probably just said this, but what's the difference between Infinite Reality and God? What's one difference between them?

Bentinho: God is the creative aspect of the potential intelligence that is innate to Infinite Reality.

Russell: And the Infinite Reality is potential.

Bentinho: Not exactly. It *has* potential, but it *is* the Infinite Reality. It is simply and totally itself. The Infinite Reality is real and ever timeless. It has the potential for creation, because it has the potential for anything and everything and nothing, all at once—because it is infinite. But at its own level, so to speak, it never changes; it never becomes anything, not even God. It is simply infinite. Perfect beyond your wildest imagination.

Russell: It's almost like Infinite Reality is a principle, like an underlying principle of everything. Whereas God is an instantiation of that.

Bentinho: I could, to some extent, agree to those terms, though I would not put it in those words myself.

Russell: So, Infinite Reality is everywhere and everything...

Bentinho: Well, *everywhere* and *everything* are terms imagined by a consciousness, by an entity. Infinite Reality is not really everywhere. God is everywhere, from the perspective of God, or when considered from a partial point of view within God's Creation. But the Absolute Reality, at its own absolute level, has no manifestation to be everywhere inside of. Something absolute cannot be everywhere, for *everywhere* implies space. Space is a concept. A concept is a manifestation—it *is*. Infinite Reality is beyond is-ness and manifestation and all consequent concepts.

Let's use the analogy of the movie *The Matrix*. If you're looking at the matrix from inside of the matrix, you could say the matrix is everywhere, right? But when you are unplugged, the matrix is gone from your experience. So you can't really say that the Reality in which you wake up is everywhere in the matrix, although the matrix does not exist apart from the Reality.

[Robert, another friend who stopped by, interjects]: Would the Absolute be like space?

Bentinho: No, that would be closer to a descriptive quality of God, although space can be an analogy for both God and, to an extent, the Absolute. But only as an analogy.

Robert: So, the Absolute is the final thing, but God would be all the objects, the people, the trees, the clouds...

Bentinho: Even the space between objects is an object, or an appearance. It's a perception produced by consciousness. Consciousness—pure, non-dual God consciousness—is the first manifestation. Inside of that, the perceptions of form and space and time and "everywhereness" begin to emerge.

Right now, you have a mind that's only used to subject-object relationships. It gets its sense of self from subject-object relationships, and it gains its imagination from subject-object relationships and conditioning. You're trying to use that faculty to produce an understanding of Reality using dream images. It's impossible—we can only approximate.

What we're talking about is an infinite, absolute, formless Reality that's beyond the consciousness that you're currently thinking through and experiencing through. And your way of imagining it is that it fills up all of space. That's like being in your dream at night and imagining and talking about the awake reality without having been there, as in, "If it's all one, it must be everywhere in my dream." But it's *not* in your dream, even though the dream does not exist apart from the awake Reality. The dream is produced and enabled inside of the awake Reality, but the awake Reality is so formless that it has nothing to do with space or omnipresence.

Before the final realization of Infinite Reality, there's an experience of the all-pervasive, omnipresent Oneness that pervades the entire Creation. But this is not the final enlightenment. The final enlightenment is the disappearance of that, and the revelation of an infinite, indescribable, complete, perfect Reality. It cannot be described, imagined or experienced in any other way than as *innately comprehending itself*. So far, I've been unable to explain it exactly; it's just absolutely wordless. No matter what I say, a concept will be generated by the listener.

Robert: And it can know itself through God...

Bentinho: In a sense, it potentiates its capacity to know itself. It increases this through the contrast of the Creation, which is one with the Creator, or God, you could say. It's an inseparable unity. The dreamer and the dream both appear simultaneously inside the infinite no-thing-ness of the Reality. In contrast to pure God consciousness, it begins to realize, "Hey, where did this pure God consciousness come from? If there is this quality of pure God consciousness, then what is before this? What's prior to this? Where did this quality of endless consciousness come from? And who is the I or the me that knows this God consciousness?"

It uses the God state of pure consciousness-beingness-bliss, which is the final state of consciousness an entity experiences in late 7th Density, as a mirror to realize its independence from Creation or God. God is the "trampoline" the entity uses to realize that, in truth, it really IS the Absolute, for that is all there really is. It uses God, the great experiencer of all, as the final mirror to see its own faceless Self. It is before manifestation or quality of any type. There's nothing beyond the Absolute Reality; it transcends all perception and perceivers.

Russell: I can follow that last sentence, I think. I have a sense of that. But I need to go back. I'm sorry but… Infinite Reality and God—these are two separate concepts?

Bentinho: As concepts in the mind, yes, you can separate them. In reality, God does not appear outside or apart from the Infinite Reality. The Infinite Reality enables, or allows for God.

Russell: Why separate these two? What do you gain by separating them?

Bentinho: It's not about what you gain, it's about what's true. I did not make this stuff up. I'm just translating truth as clearly as I know how to in description.

Russell: OK. Why can't Infinite Reality create perceptions and perceivers?

Bentinho: It can and it does, but it does so through or as God, or awareness, because in a sense, it can never leave its own level of Absoluteness. Everything would fall apart if the Absolute used its own level to become a thing. Then all things would disappear, because all things are enabled by the Absolute staying as its own Infinite Reality. If the source of a thing becomes the thing, then what happens to the thing now that its source has disappeared?

How does a CEO run a company? By hiring personnel. If the CEO truly sacrificed its own level and became a mail clerk, how would the company continue to operate? Hence there are "levels," for lack of a better word. Each level does its own job. The Absolute Reality can never become any of the levels; not even the first level, or first distortion, which is God consciousness. The Absolute can only ever stay as itself.

Russell: I realize that this requires a translation into my brain as a concept.

Bentinho: Which again, is impossible to do, but we can attempt to approximate it.

Russell: So, God is the CEO and Infinite Reality is the owner of the company?

Bentinho: Yes, that analogy can work. The CEO does not exist apart from the owner, but the owner does exist independently from the CEO and the company. There is no CEO or company without the owner, but there is whatever the owner is without the company or CEO. Of course, without the company and CEO, the owner would lose the description of *owner* because there would be nothing that he owns. But he would still be what he is.

Russell: Most people would think of "God" as both God and Infinite Reality.

Bentinho: Yes, a lot of people equate the two. I make this distinction, and one of my favorite teachers from modern times, Nisargadatta Maharaj, makes the same distinction. He says that when you realize you're not a person, that you're not a body, that you're not the individual mind, but that you're actually the Oneness, the Allness, the God consciousness, the I Am-ness out of which all perception appears—that's the first "elevation," or first enlightenment.

Then, when you realize that you're not even that, the Absolute Reality reveals itself to itself, and that's the second elevation, or second enlightenment. There aren't a lot of people who have penetrated this, so many of the descriptions out there of *enlightenment* talk about the Oneness, but they're not actually aware of the Infinite Reality beyond consciousness-isness-bliss.

What's more, those who haven't realized the distinction between the One and its oneness (God) will often use similar descriptions, even though they are pointing to God, or even merely to states of emptiness or nothingness. These states are still within God, or they are an aspect or a level of God, but they are not yet God itself at its original level. Let alone the Absolute.

It takes a very keen listener to be able to tell the difference in some of these teachings and scriptures. In fact, it takes someone who has penetrated this distinction in direct experience to truly tell the difference in these very close-sounding descriptions. This is also why we have had to clarify the same distinction so much in this dialogue.

Russell: You're going through the stages of enlightenment from the person's standpoint. I'd like to explore this from the top down, because if I was going through it, going up the way you're describing, I'd kind of want to know what I should expect from the top down. So, are you putting some limitations on God?

Bentinho: God's only limitation is that it has to be itself.

Russell: It has to be itself. And Infinite Reality does not have to be itself?

Bentinho: It does, but it is Infinite Reality, so it's not definable as a thing or a quality. Infinite Reality is not limited to the experience of consciousness or beingness. God, on the other hand, does not exist apart from consciousness or beingness; it *is* consciousness or beingness. That's its only limitation. It has to be.

Now, within that beingness or consciousness, God—which is the free will intelligence channeled from the potential inherent in the Infinite Reality—can produce an infinite number of expressions, or multiverses, universes, creations and perceptions. But it has as its root limitation that it is perception itself or beingness itself. It is not a *thing* as we know it (as in an *object*), but it is still a quality —a definable and experienceable presence.

The Infinite Reality does not have that quality as its own. If it did, it would not be absolute anymore; it would be that quality. A quality indicates partialness. Ultimately, a quality is a manifestation of some kind, and therefore loses its qualification for absoluteness or infiniteness.

That which is absolute can never appear. If it appears, it is not the Absolute. If it appears, if it has a quality, it must have a source. A quality of any kind, no matter how subtle or all-pervasive, cannot exist on its own merits.

Russell: So, Infinite Reality does not need consciousness.

Bentinho: Correct.

Russell: Where do the laws of physics fit in?

Bentinho: Those are the very outer aspects of God; they pretty much come last. They are not very fundamental to the spiritual journey, except as organizational principles in certain densities that help structure the experience within which a linear entity has to grow and learn.

Russell: And that's within God consciousness.

Bentinho: Anything perceivable is within the universal "bubble" of God consciousness, including the illusion of physics.

Russell: OK. Maybe this is where I'm stuck, and maybe it's because you can't explain it or it can't be put into words. You've got Infinite Reality, and right below that is consciousness, or God, which includes the law of physics. And there could be different laws of physics in different universes. So, the part that's left is the non-conscious part of Infinite Reality, the part that is not included in God.

Bentinho: Let me rephrase what you said and see if this is what you mean. God is not aware of the Infinite Reality, but the Infinite Reality is aware of God. So, God has the ability to know itself, but it cannot know the Infinite Reality with its own consciousness. The moment God knows the Infinite Reality, it has actually shifted into *being* the Infinite Reality once again, and its job as God is revoked. Its Creation ends. Then, only the one Infinite Reality is. God has exited through the black hole, and now IS the Infinite Reality. And thus its Creation "ends" because its sustainer—God—is gone. The substratum has left the building. I guess you could say at this stage that the building itself has left the building. Haha.

Russell: [Russell begins to draw again.] OK, so this is Infinite Reality, continuous Reality. And this is God, which is consciousness…

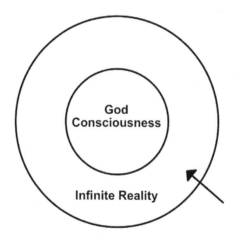

Bentinho: God is the experiencer, beingness, consciousness, sentience, awareness.

Russell: What I want to know is, what's in there? [Russell points to Infinite Reality.]

Bentinho: What's in there?

Russell: Yeah.

Bentinho: Nothing, because you're asking for a perception, for an experience or quality. But the Absolute is that which enables the awareness of all perception, yet remains itself timelessly beyond any perception. So, no perception, or no thing, is "in" here. Only its own Infiniteness is "there."

Russell: Infinite Reality is my big circle. God is a subset of that—consciousness plus a couple of other terms. I want to know what is in Infinite Reality that God is not part of. That is still my question.

Bentinho: The infinite, formless Reality beyond experiencing.

Russell: Beyond whose experience?

Bentinho: Beyond God's experience.

Russell: So, there is stuff going on beyond God's experience?

Bentinho: Not *stuff*, because anything that is stuff is a subset of consciousness.

Russell: OK, so what's there?

Bentinho: The infinite, absolute, indescribable, unimaginable Reality; the Reality out of which anything perceivable—the Grand Illusion—is seemingly enabled to appear to consciousness. This is why it uses presence or consciousness or beingness—so that ultimately, in the final stage of consciousness' evolution, it can know itself in contrast to that. So, if this consciousness includes everything that could ever be experienced, and at some point… Let's draw it like this:

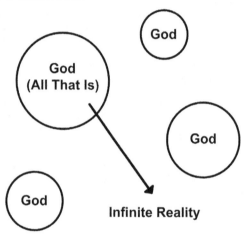

Bentinho: The Infinite Reality is the space, you could say. Inside of that, there is the God consciousness—the bubble.

Russell: So, Infinite Reality is the sheet of paper?

Bentinho: Yes, in this analogy, Infinite Reality is the paper itself.

Russell: This piece of paper?

Bentinho: Yes, but you're trying to make it into *something* again. Any something is a perception that arises because of God. God is the experiencer of all that is, of all that could ever be. God's only limitation is is-ness, consciousness or beingness.

Russell: Is what?

Bentinho: Is-ness, consciousness or beingness. God's only limitation is that it has to be. What's outside of this is *non-beingness*, you could say, or rather: *beyond-beingness*. But it's still the Infinite Reality, so it's not like it doesn't exist. It gets really hard to talk about this.

Russell: Is the Infinite Reality an actual thing, or just potential?

Bentinho: Saying that is like trying to put the Infinite Reality somewhere in the bubble of God. You're trying to turn the Infinite Reality into a perceivable thing.

Russell: Right. And so I still...

Bentinho: You still don't get it.

Russell: I still don't get it! [Laughter]

Bentinho: The mind will never get it! It's kind of a joke. You have to go beyond the mind, and even beyond consciousness itself, to realize it.

Russell: If God is everything I can perceive or think of or experience...

Bentinho: Including the experience of itself, which is the experience of pure beingness with no space-time limitations—just pure, eternal, locationless is-ness. That's the final *experience*. The Infinite Reality is what this first, final, and truly *only* experience (because we never don't experience beingness) is rested in or upon. God is the first addition to the infinite perfection of the one Infinite Reality. God is the first "experienceable," the first distinction, if you will, between its original stateless state and itself as an experienceable.

Russell: So, the Infinite Reality is something that is not; it does not have this is-ness.

Bentinho: Correct. And yet it's the only real reality.

Russell: Infinite Reality is the only real reality.

Bentinho: Yes. All else is a play of perceptions within the primary perception, which is consciousness. Consciousness is the subtlest and first perception; all other perceivables (or forms) are its consequent production, organization, expression or effects.

Russell: You almost can't describe it positively; you can only describe it negatively.

Bentinho: Yes! Very nice! That's why those very rare teachings about the Infinite Reality are often presented in a negating style, "I am not this, I am not that..."

Russell: You're basically throwing out everything.

Bentinho: Exactly. When you keep negating objects, what you end up with is the experience of the "God bubble" itself. This is the substratum of experience itself. It is the experiencer, the pure beingness-consciousness. When you're able to maintain that...

Russell: Wait! This is important. So, the first step is to understand and sense God consciousness.

Bentinho: Yes. The first step is to perceive beingness or presence or consciousness by giving away all perceptions of objects. Then you become the subject itself, the universal subject, which is pure is-ness, beingness, consciousness. If you are able to maintain that for long enough, you can begin to awaken even deeper, with a faculty that is not the mind. It is actually Infinite Reality awakening to itself in contrast to God consciousness.

Russell: Let me rephrase this. I think this is kind of exciting! So, you kind of learn little pieces of the God bubble —experiences, perceptions, and knowledge—and you sense into it more and more to get the whole picture... and then, you throw it all out! [Russell makes an excited swoop of his arm in the air, with a smile on his face like he just figured something out. An aha! moment for Russell!]

Bentinho: Correct my friend! Fuck yes!

Russell: That's really cool!

Bentinho: One of my most direct teachings when it comes to guiding people to a sense—at least an intuitive sense, much more rarely a full-blown realization—of the Absolute Reality is this: Whatever perception comes up for you, whatever is registered in your consciousness—throw it in the "trash bin" of God, or *I am*. Give it back to the beingness. Say to yourself, "This all belongs to beingness, to God, to the *Great I Am*."

This way, all of the individuated perspectives are given back, or surrendered, to the wholeness of God, enabling you to experience the God essence state more and more vividly, more and more brightly. Then, after maturing in this God consciousness—soaking in it like you would soak your body in a long, warm bath—you deny that very God consciousness completely. You ignore it and see what remains without even that pure essential beingness. What is revealed is your Self—you without any additions; Infinity Reality. What follows is indescribable.

Russell: It makes sense that you can't explain it very well with words.

Bentinho: Right! Thanks, I gave it a shot!

Russell: So, have you done that? Have you gone to the point where you were able to toss it all out?

Bentinho: Yes, multiple times exclusively or entirely. And virtually all the time intuitively, simultaneous to everything else I witness and/or engage in.

Russell: And then the question is whether you stay there at the top.

Bentinho: Yes, that's perhaps *the* question.

Russell [to Suzie, a friend]: Have you understood this?

Suzie: Yeah. It happened in The Sedona Experiment for the first time for me.

Bentinho: [After some pause...] Cool! Awesome Russell! I'm impressed.

Russell: You stayed with me on it!

Bentinho: This is why I still choose to also be "here."

Russell: I have another question. I kind of have a sense that there are more levels. Are there?

Bentinho: There is only the Absolute, the Infinite Reality. There are no levels here anymore. It's stateless; it's level-less. That's why I use the word *absolute*—because there is nothing beyond it; it is the Infinite.

Russell: You were talking about the stages of enlightenment...

Bentinho: That's all inside of the God experience—which is where the densities of consciousness exist. You already have a denser awareness of self, of beingness, than let's say, a plant. A plant would be classified as a 2nd Density life form for consciousness to latch onto, so to speak, in order to experience itself as, for example, tree-ness, and to learn what it learns instinctively in that state. In 3rd Density, you already have a higher density of self awareness than that. Then there are 4th, 5th, 6th and 7th Densities respectively, each with their own main and secondary focal points or lessons. 7th Density is the density of allness; of experientially becoming one with the essence of all that is—God consciousness. It is the surrender of the individual soul to the allness of God.

And at the end of 7th Density, there is what I call the *black hole*. When you have accumulated enough "spiritual mass," your beingness-totality collapses in on itself, and all of consciousness disappears back into the Infinite Reality, where nothing ever happened or appeared. From our 3rd Density point of view, we symbolically perceive this as the black hole—that which absorbs all light at the end of a major cycle of experience.

So, a question could be: "What's beyond the black hole when all the light is reabsorbed?" I've also had experiences of this black hole phenomenon specifically, that's why I sometimes use it as an analogy.

Russell: Well, that's your "white hole" then. That's your Big Bang, right?

Bentinho: The *white hole* would be the 1st Density or Big Bang of the next Creation or *octave* of illusory vibrations. A new multiverse, if you will.

For a timeless amount of timelessness, there is just the Infinite Reality. And then somehow, due to some mysterious potential, which is simultaneous to this because there is no time, there is the creation of another octave—another illusion, another God (or free will intelligence, or consciousness) to govern and direct its flow and patterns. Another universe, another Creation. Because in an Infinite Reality, why not have infinite Creations?

Russell: Well yeah, you gotta have infinite universes! [Bentinho chuckles] How many dimensions are there? Are there an infinite number of dimensions?

Bentinho: Depending a little bit on what you mean by "dimensions," I would say there are an infinite number of dimensions, or layers/levels inside of Creation, but there are seven main dimensions, or densities, that are distinct enough in their density of light to generate a threshold between them. The 8th Density is sort of symbolic in my experience, being the Absolute Reality. It's really not a manifest dimension in my view; it's more like a gap between octaves, or a "void" of pure Infinite Reality between the illusions of Creations. It is, in this way, the Absolute space beyond all manifest spaces.

Russell: My logic gets it! At least part of it. Probably not all of it.

Bentinho: Wooo! That's great!

Robert: So, within the Absolute there are other expressions of God, or other octaves? Other distortions, like this one?

Bentinho: Yes. From the Absolute, I've glimpsed or sensed other "Creation bubbles," if you will. Like miniature specs or bubbles of light, each containing an entire Creation, floating in an infinite perfection, and impossible to describe to consciousness. The Absolute is never affected in the slightest by any of these Creations. Each of these bubbles or specs of light are hardly noticeable from the Absolute, unless focused upon and zoomed-in on using the innate ability of awareness to focus itself. Then, such a bubble or Creation becomes "bigger" if you will, and apparently more real, as it zips into focus.

Perhaps compare it to putting on virtual reality (VR) goggles. When you're outside of the virtual reality, the reality inside the VR goggles appears as non-existent to you because you're not perceiving the illusion. But as you put on the goggles, a veil of perception is pulled over your eyes and now, all of a sudden, what was not even felt or sensed as existent, appears in-full, as if it exists. It appears to be.

It's comparable to other galaxies within the space of our known universe or octave of Creation. But really, the space, with all of its billions of galaxies, only exists inside of the God consciousness or VR goggles. The Absolute would be akin to putting down the goggles and being that which remains.

Russell: It feels like the rest is just details.

Bentinho: Yeah, nice! Congrats, man! Thanks for your interest—this has been great.

CONVERSATION 3:

PERCEPTION, TRUTH & LEVELS OF CONSCIOUSNESS

Russell: First, I just want to thank Bentinho for meeting with me today. He has been texting me, bugging me, and wanting to know what the meaning and essence of life is, and I don't really know what the difference is between these two things.

I want to bring up St. Augustine. St. Augustine wrote a lot about time and he was also trying to figure out the Bible. He thought about how God created the universe, and what was before that. What was there before God created the universe? Beyond Earth, he acknowledges the stars and the sun, and of course he thought the Earth was at the center of it. So, his problem was...

Bentinho: That he was a Christian? [Laughter]

Russell: The problem was that he was a Christian! Hahaha.

Yeah, he was a believer, a really hard core believer, pretty much from birth. His mother was very religious and prayed for him everyday. His father was a non-believer who didn't really care about religion; he just wanted his son to succeed in the world. He wanted him to get a good education.

Bentinho: Can you remember what time frame this was?

Russell: Augustine was born in 354 AD.

Bentinho: That's specific; I like it. 354 AD.

Russell: He had a very religious mother, and he says that he was very "lustful" as a kid and acted on that.

Bentinho: Lustful like aggressive or sexual?

Russell: Sexual. Around the age of 18 or 19 or 20, he started an affair with a woman, and he kept it going for about 10 years. He had a kid with her, a son, and every day his mother would pray for his soul. She wanted him to "marry up" and felt that this woman he was having a relationship with wasn't good enough for him. So, when he was 28-years-old or so, his mother came to Rome and basically got him engaged to another girl. But the girl wasn't old enough to marry yet, so he had to wait. The marrying age in Rome at the time was 12, and he was engaged to a 10-year-old.

Bentinho: Wow.

Russell: This girl was someone of a higher class who was appropriate for him, according to his mother.

Bentinho: So, he was 28 then?

Russell: He was 28. He had still not accepted Jesus as his saviour. He believed in Jesus, but he wasn't ready to accept him or to live the way Jesus would expect him to live. His will was weak at that point.

So anyway, he sends the mother of his son back to North Africa, where she was born. He kept the boy. And since he had two years to wait until he could marry the girl his mother picked out, he found another mistress. [Laughter]

Right before he was supposed to be married, he accepted the Catholic faith and became celibate from then on; from about age 30 on. So, he didn't marry her. He became very religious. But he always felt that he had sinned and that he was wicked, until he really accepted God and Jesus. And then he wrote like a madman.

Bentinho: He wrote like a madman?

Russell: Yeah. He basically wrote his autobiography, which was probably the first serious autobiography in Western literature. In his book, he confessed to many of his sins—his lustful behavior and all that.

Bentinho: Have you read this autobiography?

Russell: Yes, it's called *Confessions*. The philosophy of the Catholic Church, or Christianity, was based on his writings for 900 years.

Bentinho: Wait—say that again. That's a pretty bold statement.

Russell: The philosophy of Christianity was based on his interpretations for about 900 years.

Bentinho: His interpretations of the Bible?

Russell: Yeah, about what God is, the trinity, and so on.

Bentinho: OK.

Russell: Augustine was a philosopher. He tried to be as rational and logical, as well as (kind of) scientific, as he could be. But there was never any doubt that God created the universe, that God created everything, and that Jesus was the son of God.

Bentinho: God forbid!

Russell: God forbid! The question of the trinity... well, that was a big mystery. How could the Father, the Son, and the Holy Spirit be separate but one?

Bentinho: Now we're getting into my territory.

Russell: Is that your territory?

Bentinho: Yeah, sort of. The many paradoxes created by the simultaneity of unity and diversity, or multiplicity.

Russell: One of the issues that came up for him was that Jesus was begotten by God, so Jesus could be thought of as the Son of God. But the Holy Spirit was also begotten by God, and if they are "all for one and one for all," like the three musketeers, then why wasn't the Holy Spirit considered the Son of God, as well? I actually don't know what his answer was, since I'm only half-way through his book on the trinity.

Bentinho: Was this a separate book or was it part of his autobiography?

Russell: It's a separate book.

What he was trying to explain is that individuals have a trinity within them, which is similar to the Christian trinity. The trinity within, he says, is the mind, knowledge and love. So, for the mind to know itself, it has to have true knowledge and love. And both of those are God. God is perfect knowledge and God is the greatest love. Infinite love and infinite knowledge. The more the mind knows itself, the closer it gets to God.

Bentinho: So, a couple of questions.

Russell: OK.

Bentinho: Did he separate mind and knowledge? Did he say they are two different things?

Russell: It's like the Father and the Son.

Bentinho: Ah.

Russell: That's his point.

Bentinho: Right. So, according to him, there is a mind apart from knowledge—even though it is not separate?

Can there be mind with no knowledge in his view? Or is knowledge mind? Or does he not specify that?

Russell: For the mind to know itself and get close to God, it needs knowledge. It needs true knowledge.

Bentinho: And by "knowledge" does he mean knowledge of concepts, or does he mean the experiential knowledge of self—the self awareness kind of knowledge?

Russell: I don't understand him well enough right now to answer that for him, but I don't think it's factual. I think it's the...

Bentinho: The spiritual knowledge of self.

Russell: I was wondering about that too, and I don't know, based on what I have read so far.

Bentinho: Maybe later on in the book.

Russell: Maybe. Or maybe he doesn't go over that. One thing he is doing is defining. He defines *God* as *ultimate*— ultimate knowledge and ultimate love—and he says the highest essence of mind is ultimate knowledge and ultimate love. So, he defines them to be sort of the same. I think there is a circular argument there; that's what he's doing.

Bentinho: Aha.

Russell: The argument he's trying to make is that people have, within their own self and their own mind, something similar to the holy trinity. And I don't know if that argument works yet. Do you teach something related to that?

Bentinho: Uhmm yeah... my brand is called "Trinfinity."

Russell: Haha, right!

Bentinho: Trinfinity: infinite trinity, or alternatively, you could say a three-faceted infinity.

What I was mostly referring to is the idea of how things can be seen as separate, and yet somehow be one, simultaneously. The idea that things can exist in both perceptual domains simultaneously: the domain of diversity, separation, and multiplicity and the domain of Oneness. Both are true, and this paradox is often addressed in my work. Obviously, not specifically as it refers to God, the Son and the Holy Spirit. Or at least not in those terms and not based on any particular religion.

Russell: I know I've asked you this before, but what are the three things in your trinity, or Trinfinity?

Bentinho: A trinity is applicable to many aspects of our experience, but originally, when I came up with this name the main pillars were:

1. The individual consciousness.

2. The presence of God or consciousness itself. Some people might call this "the field," or a sort of oceanic Oneness that is the root substratum, the root

intelligence or the God principle that constitutes and underlies every individual.

3. The Absolute or Infinite Reality. We discussed this previously; I hope you remember your conclusion about it!

Russell: Haha!

Bentinho: If not, we have it on tape. I will remind you. In fact, I will send you the book. [Laughter]

Russell: I'll have to buy the book! [Laughter]

Bentinho: Our book. You will have to buy our book!

Russell: Haha, right! OK, so there is the individual consciousness...

Bentinho: There is the individual consciousness, the universal consciousness, and the original source before any of it. And the line in the Trinfinity symbol that connects the three "circles," or aspects, is represented by awareness, or the ability to navigate between these seemingly distinct expressions of this Oneness. Awareness is also known as free will, though not "free will" as is often defined in a more limiting, personal way. Free will rather as in the ability to be, to know, to choose and to direct one's self.

Russell: OK, but these aren't like three separate circles, a circle within a circle within a circle, right?

Bentinho: No. You know the infinity symbol, which looks like a sideways 8? The trinfinity symbol is basically that, but with three loops instead of two. Like this. [Bentinho draws the Trinfinity symbol.]

Russell: Right. I remember this now, from one of our previous conversations.

Bentinho: So, the line is the free agency of awareness which, with training, has the ability to zoom-in on the individual, or zoom-out to the substratum experience (the true knowledge of God), or to go beyond it altogether and penetrate The Absolute, or Infinite Reality. The line is what connects these three "experiences."

Russell: So, you're not saying that individual consciousness is the same as the universal consciousness...

Bentinho: In essence they are the same, but they are experienced as quite different. But they are not separate, just as a dream does not exist separately from the dreamer. Yet to experience a dream without awareness of the dreamer feels very different than to experience it being aware of the dreamer. So they are different states of consciousness, yet never separate from one another.

Russell: Let's say there are three people in the world. Three aware people.

Bentinho: Who's the third? I thought only you and I existed right now.

Russell: I don't know who the third is, but I hope they bring us food! [Laughter]

Bentinho: Let's hope the third person in existence is a woman, or mankind is doomed.

Russell: Indeed! OK then, let's say there are four people in the world.

Bentinho: What? No! That eliminates the trinity!

Russell: OK, it's all the same. Let's just say there are two people—you and me. I think I can do it with that. So, is your awareness, your consciousness, different than my consciousness? And I'm going to be a little worried if it's not. [Laughter]

Bentinho: Yes and no.

Russell: Yes and no?

Bentinho: This is why I remarked that we are now getting into "my territory"—because of these types of paradoxes regarding a simultaneity of oneness and diversity. Within the realm of Creation, or this Great Illusion, there are many co-existing truths, which to the linear, 3D-oriented mind seem like opposites or contradictions, when in essence there is no friction between any of them.

It takes the transcendence of the conventional mind to

grasp the simultaneity of these types of laws or truths. So yes, on an expression level, there is a difference between our consciousnesses, but ultimately, there is not. Both statements are true within their own perceptual domains of being. Even if one may be illusory and the other not.

Russell: And this is because we are all part of the same universal consciousness. Is that correct? Is that how we are the same?

Bentinho: Yes. And you could make it an even stronger statement by saying that our individual expressions would not exist without that universal consciousness. One's individual consciousness completely depends upon the universal consciousness. We are distinct, but not substantially or essentially independent from one another, nor independent from the totality-field of consciousness. Individual consciousness was not born out of nothing. It arose out of this universal consciousness, if we want to call it that for now. Or you could say God, or All That Is.

Russell: Let's assume that I make a balloon, a red balloon. Well, I don't make it, I just blow up a red balloon with air.

Bentinho: You bought it?

Russell: No, you bought it. But I used an air pump to fill it and I tied it. I have a red one; what color do you want yours to be?

Bentinho: Blue.

Russell: OK, blue. Now both balloons are filled with the same air that is around us; they are part of it.

Bentinho: Exactly.

Russell: But they are clearly separate. There is air inside of one red latex balloon (or whatever balloons are made out of; plastic, latex, I don't know!) and there is air inside of one blue balloon. There is one balloon over here and one over there. I could even pop one of them.

There are two separate balloons, but they are both part of the "universal whole of air." Now this is different than Augustine's trinity, because he wants to say that, even though they are different—and the Son was begotten of the Father—they are actually the same; there is no way to tell them apart. They are infinite, and they both have all of the qualities—infinite goodness, infinite knowledge, and so on. I don't know if the balloon analogy works or not, but it's different than Augustine's Christian trinity.

Bentinho: In a sense it works, but it depends on the level of perception we experience. There is an all-inclusive unity or simultaneity existing all at once, and it consists of different levels of perception. From each level of perception, different things appear to be true at different times.

You can even see this on a human scale. For example, if you ask a child about a complex issue, he or she will likely only be able to see and describe the surface of it, but what they see and describe about the issue is most likely correct in terms of what is being observed and stated, as in "I see this, I see that..." Even though it's not the whole picture, that doesn't make the observation from the child's level untrue. It's just not the whole picture, and it's being seen from a certain level of understanding.

If you were to go deeper into the balloon analogy, where you have your own consciousness and I have my own consciousness, then from the outside, from the perspective of the balloon, there is separation there. But from the perspective of the air, it is the same air in both balloons, and it is indistinguishable. So, I don't fully disagree.

I don't know how St. Augustine felt about this, but I would add the acknowledgement that, from a different level of consciousness or perception, there is a very observable distinction that is different in functionality. And it can be appreciated as such, knowing that it is not *ultimately* true, but rather that it is *relatively* true.

This is valuable to me because, in an all-inclusive unity, which this existence definitely is, in my experience, all aspects of it must be appreciated, even if seen to be only partially true, or not ultimately true. One can dismiss a lower level of truth and go beyond it, but ultimately, one no longer needs to resist a lower level of truth in order to experience a higher level of truth. In true unity, there is simultaneity of All That Is, and with that comes an equanimity and appreciation of all things as being the one Infinite Reality.

Russell: Actually, I like that better than Augustine's description! So far, I don't believe he has been able to prove what he's trying to prove—that God and the Son are the same, even though somehow they are conceptually different. I relate more to your description.

Bentinho: Well, we've got 1600 years on him...

Russell: Are any of these levels more true than the other levels? Are they all true?

Bentinho: Here is the paradox within the paradox—yes and no! It's like an infinite fractal of paradox. The paradox is always resolved, if you can accept it. If you can't accept the paradox, then it will never be resolved, because there is always a paradox inside the paradox from the limited, linear mind's point of view. I've noticed this with these types of questions. The paradoxical questions don't ever have to end for as long as they are entertained.

So, I would say yes, there are truer levels of perception where the perceptions of life are less distorted than at other levels. And yet, the distorted levels of perception are also, in essence, inseparable from the Creator's perception of itself. Whether the Creator sees itself clearly in one area of its Creation and unclearly through another expression or individuation of itself, both are still the Creator knowing itself.

So in a way, they are to be valued as equally valid to any other level of perception, even though one does not have to ascribe to the distorted perception or stay stuck there. Appreciation does not mean to indulge or identify with it; it simply means we can (and ultimately will) appreciate illusion as being part of the Creator's exploration of itself.

However, from a mathematical point of view (if you will), or from a universal-scale point of view (if you will), or from the level of purity or wholeness (if you will), the more whole perspective would be to see the Oneness over the multiplicity. In that sense, the Oneness is more true than the illusion of separation. But because there is only one Oneness, an entity who is at the level of complete Oneness would have an innate and natural appreciation of each lesser point of view as being part of the whole—inseparably so. There would be an appreciation of it as if that perspective too, is the Creator, in all of its fullness. And again, this appreciation of illusion does not mean one is blinded by or bound to that illusion, or that one believes it to be true.

Russell: You mentioned illusion. So, let's just say, at the lowest level, where I live... [Laughter]

Bentinho: Just you and me... down here on Earth, without food or pleasant company! [Laughter]

Russell: According to my philosophy reading, a classic analogy for illusion that is sometimes spoken of is a stick that's halfway immersed in water. The stick looks bent, because the water refracts the light differently than the air does. So, is that illusion real? Is it true? In a sense it's true, but if you pull the stick out of the water, it will not be bent.

Bentinho: Nice. I like that analogy. I would say it's true as an *experience*, because it's truly experienced in that way. The perception is a truly valid perception as a perception, but it might not be mathematically, structurally or me-chanically correct, so it may be a distorted perception. Yet the experience of that perception is as valid as any other experience of perception that the Creator is having of itself within this Great Illusion through an individuated, distorted view.

To create a hierarchy of which perception within the Great Illusion is more valid than another is helpful, if provided by a master with clarity and a structure designed to help the seeker advance. Such a structure of advancement can be helpful, at least to the beginning and intermediate seeker. However, at the higher levels of communion with the universal Beingness, an unconditional love, clarity and transcendence from individuated points of view begins to loosen up these opposites, polarities and contradictions. Thus, at the higher levels, the paradox is experientially resolved for the seeker of God, and the obviousness of unity begins to outshine the apparent (but ultimately illusory) nature of separate realities.

Russell: But if you look at it from a more universal perspective, is that illusion true? Or does it just fall away somehow?

Bentinho: Say that again...

Russell: If I look at it scientifically, I would say it's an illusion. It's not true; the stick is not bent. Although I also agree that, based on the experience of it, it looks as if it's bent. So, I can say that the *experience* of seeing it as a bent stick is true, but the stick is not *actually* bent, so there is a disconnect there.

Now, if I were to look at it from a higher level, from a universal consciousness level, would it add anything to what I just said from a scientific angle? Does it give me any additional insight if I look at it from a universal level? Maybe that doesn't make any sense... I'll try it a different way; in a more dialectic way of reasoning about things.

Bentinho: What's the definition of *dialectic*?

Russell: It's a way of contrasting things. Karl Marx used the term a lot. You take one thing that you think is a fact and find something that disagrees with it. Then you compare these two things. Dialectically, you compare these two things, and you come to a higher understanding that incorporates both of them.

Bentinho: Nice.

Russell: So, for that concept—the stick looks bent but the stick is not bent—I'm wondering if there is a synthesis of these two facts that can be attained if you go higher in consciousness.

Bentinho: What I can say is that, as you "go higher in consciousness," so to speak, the whole predicament loses its value. It is replaced by an appreciation of the multiplicity of experience, all being equally valid. At the same time, however, there is a hierarchy of truthfulness, or the distortedness/undistortedness of perception, knowledge, or awareness. If you go high enough in consciousness, the whole predicament disappears; it simply no longer occupies your interest, and instinctively and directly, the lesser truths are integrated. They are included in a larger body of knowledge which indeed has synthesized or resolved the paradox.

As you go higher in consciousness, my experience (which is corroborated by others who have claimed to go higher in consciousness) is that the understanding of a mechanically true, objective universe that independently and physically exists on its own, apart from consciousness, is resolved. When that is resolved...

Russell: When that is resolved?

Bentinho: Yeah, when it is resolved it disappears. It is no longer seen to be the way that it appears on the more partial levels of consciousness. What is seen is that there are an infinite number of parallel expressions, which are all equally purposeful in that they all express the one infinite God, Creator, or Source Intelligence in every way possible. Every perception performs its duty, whether it does so consciously or unconsciously, by being a useful extension, expansion or manifestation of the infinite potential of the Creator knowing itself, experiencing itself, expressing itself, and creating all these illusions or hallucinations out of its own beingness.

The question is no longer about trying to prove whether the stick is straight or if it's bent at an angle. What I see is that, even if the stick is mechanically straight and it just appears to be bent because of the water, the straight stick, as well as the bent stick, only exist as perceptions within consciousness. Therefore, neither one is necessarily more true, ultimately.

You could then add a layer of *relative* truthfulness to this. We all have some degree of consensus experience of this collective dimension that we call "planet Earth" because we are all perceiving, to some extent, similar portions of the hallucination. So, you could say that conceptually, within a certain probable system of a reality that has certain parameters (such as planet Earth), it is more mathematically or mechanically correct that the stick is actually straight. And within this paradigm, the illusion of the stick being bent is created by the water.

But the higher you go in consciousness, the more you see that this whole probable system itself is also an illusion. You see that the empirical universe and empirical truths are but an agreement in consciousness only, and that in truth, there is no stick, there is no water, and there is no universe. I suppose there is also no spoon. And come to think of it, there still isn't any food or pleasant company either...

Russell: [Laughter] So it's all consciousness.

Bentinho: Right. Trying to prove that one thing is more true than another thing kind of loses its appeal. Is one perception within your dream at night ultimately more true than another perception? Because the idea that there's an empirical universe—an independently existent Creation—dissolves, and that changes the whole Gestalt of philosophy and investigation and interests.

Russell: Right, so within this material world, or maybe that's not a good word...

Bentinho: Within this level of perception where the world seems material...

Russell: Right, some illusions are more consistent with the system that...

Bentinho: You can speak in terms of probabilities and you can speak of consistencies within agreements, etc. Certain agreements are more consistent than—or we could say, form the container for—smaller agreements that are less consistent. But from a higher level of consciousness, none of them can ultimately be said to be "more true" because ultimately none of them are true. And yet they are all equally valid as expressions, as hallucinations, as experiences of the Oneness. These are all provided by the Oneness to itself, in a variety of temporarily valuable, yet illusory, ways. This way of seeing it is the result of having experientially resolved—or transcended—the duality or illusion of separation.

Russell: So, for someone like me... [laughter] who takes reality as he sees it, I could get into trouble with this.

Bentinho: Uh huh. Nice catch.

Russell: What do I gain or lose... I don't even know what I am saying now, but what do I gain or lose by not... what if, in my worldview there is no universal consciousness. What do I...

Bentinho: Then you are stuck, to an extent, within the paradigm to which you limit your perception.

Russell: Would I lose some personal experiences if I can't or won't connect with the Oneness?

Bentinho: Well, you would lose the ability to know the truth of the matter. Like, there's a guy on a tropical island who puts a stick in the water, and he tells you he doesn't believe there is a straight stick. He wants to figure out the truth of the matter without believing that there could be a straight stick. It's kind of like that when you say to me, "I want to get to the bottom of whatever this is, but what if I don't believe that the universe exists inside of consciousness?"

To me, that's a greatly limited investigation of truth, just as on a more relative level, it would be a greatly limited investigation of truth if the guy on the tropical island was not interested in knowing the stick outside of the water. He wants to figure out the truth about the stick, but he refuses to pull it out of the water.

Russell: I can come up with some consequences of believing that the stick is bent when actually it is not. For example, the person may have to take it out of the water to measure the shortest distance between two points. The distance would be shorter with a straight stick. I would have to work on the analogy, but I think I could come up with something, an experiment, where if a person thinks the stick is really bent when it's in the water, it wouldn't obey the laws on this planet.

Bentinho: Uh huh.

Russell: If you want me to think really hard, I could try to come up with that. I think I could show that it's internally inconsistent in this material world.

Bentinho: But what if that person still would not accept that theology?

Russell: Someone might think that if I put a penny in a swimming pool, it's not going to sink to the bottom. So I put a penny in the pool, and it goes to the bottom. Now they may not believe that—OK. [Laughter] They might think that they can walk across the surface of the swimming pool, and I'll say, "No, I don't think you can, as that goes against physics as I understand it." If they try to do it and they sink into the water, they should accept that they weren't able to do it. So that proves my point—they couldn't do it.

Bentinho: What is the point behind or before that?

Russell: Well, I guess what I am saying is that...

Bentinho: Are we still discussing the point about how we can continue a dialogue like this without you believing or accepting that the universe depends on consciousness, or that perception depends on...

Russell: Yeah, I'm still trying to figure out what I lose by not accepting it.

Bentinho: Everything! [Laughter] The ability to grok the truth of existence, most of all.

Russell: I lose access to the truth.

Bentinho: Currently, from this level of perception with which you are most familiar, we can only speculate and observe localized phenomena, because we are separating out the intellect. Maybe that's too strong of a statement and is not absolutely true, but in a sense, we are separating the intellect from the nature of All That Is. We are trying to understand the nature of All That Is with this inherently limited component of nature (the intellect), and we're going to be limited to the means that we deploy. Disbelief in the nature of consciousness as the constitution of the ground of All That Is will limit us to our senses and the intellect. So yeah, I think it's greatly limiting in our investigation of what's true. And it assumes that the truth is within the realm of the senses or the intellect. To an extent it assumes that.

Russell: OK.

Bentinho: Right? Because if you believe there's a truth that exists apart from the intellect and the senses, a truth that is not observable or understandable by the senses or the intellect, then you are one step closer to expanding the tools that you could deploy.

Russell: What was that?

Bentinho: We are expanding upon the toolbox that we have. We're trying our best to put this into an intellectual framework, but no matter how accurate the intellectual framework is, it will never be the truth. It will always be an image, a collection of sensory data, thought processes, reasoning... which is obviously not the truth itself. It is the attempt to use these tools to recreate an *image* of the truth.

To me, understanding the nature of consciousness and how it may be constituting reality or perception in general, is kind of crucial in being able to get to know the truth, which you could call God or the mystery of life. In my experience, this just cannot be grokked by the intellect and the senses. So then, we're limiting our understanding and experience to that realm.

I enjoy creating images that resemble the truth, too. The main purpose for this in my work is that, if an entity is able to have a more accurate representation of the truth, or the mystery, then they are better able to access new senses, new perceptions, or new levels of consciousness that are not limited to the intellect or the senses as we know them. I'm using an intellectual framework to give people a roadmap to find the edge of their intellect, and hopefully, to find the will and the interest to explore what is beyond that edge.

In my experience, it's only been after I have gone beyond the intellect that I have a more intimate perception of what I'm sharing here today, even if I already had the intellectual framework figured out to a degree before transcending the mind and the senses. It's perhaps similar to you approaching the person with the stick in the water and pulling the stick out of the water for him. And the person goes, "Ah, OK. I really saw it as bent, but now I understand that it's straight." It's kind of similar to that.

From my paradigm, your stance is limiting because the

truth cannot be found with the senses or the mind. We can still talk about these things and have a really good time, but that's what you're missing out on—the more intimate, experiential, spiritual, ultimate knowledge of God, Life, Existence. Call this what you will.

Russell: That makes sense. I like the way you brought the analogy of the stick back into the conversation.

So, the connection between higher consciousness and this world... What is that connection? Is it meditation or experiences? Is it drugs? Intuition?

Bentinho: All of these things can work. I don't particularly recommend drugs, and have never been big on using them myself, but people seem to have opened certain perceptions or levels of consciousness through them. In the ideal case, it's the combination of intuition, meditation and will. I would say it starts with a will to know; the desire to know the truth. And that desire must be coupled with an intuitive sense, in order to become strong enough to transcend the realm of the senses and the intellect.

If the person in your analogy sees the stick bent in the water, he is not wrong. Similarly, I also see what you're seeing when you're explaining intellectually sound things. I agree with what you are seeing; I see it too. I understand your world, or rather: your perception of life.

But back to the stick analogy... If the person doesn't have an intuition that maybe this is not the whole truth, and if the person doesn't have sufficient will or interest to find out the truth—if the person is complacent or satisfied or happy with what they're seeing and their understanding of what they are seeing—then their will won't become strong enough to consider pulling the stick out of the water.

But if the intuition is strong, and one is not satisfied with just what one sees at present, it will reinforce the will to explore beyond the familiar means of perceiving. If the will gets stronger, then the intuition will be activated and will be drawn upon, relied upon more, and trusted more than one trusts one's senses or thoughts.

The stronger the will to know the truth becomes, the more rapidly you'll find the limitations of the tools you've been using so far. If your will or desire is not very strong and / or your intuition is not yet activated (or relied upon or trusted), then you won't be bothered by the limits of the intellect and the senses. Nor will you seek to find their limits, because you're not looking for anything else. Would you agree?

Russell: Yeah, I think so too.

Bentinho: When these two elements are in place—the will to know what is beyond one's current paradigm and an appreciation of an intelligence that transcends the tools you have used so far (mainly the senses and the intellect or reasoning)—if these combine, then meditation can help accelerate it. The prerequisite to having a good meditation is true curiosity, or will, and some degree of faith that there is an intelligence or a truth beyond what's obvious to you now, and the faith that this intelligence can somehow be accessed by you.

So, meditation is a method that can help accelerate this. But it is not necessarily needed. There are people who have penetrated very deeply into subjective levels of truth, or into experiential perceptions of existence that don't seem to fit into the paradigm of the intellect and the senses, who haven't adopted any formal meditation practice. By the sheer strength of their desire to know, and/or by their connection to their intuition, or their appreciation of that "gut feeling," they have been able to penetrate into the perceptions they have been seeking. You will find what you seek, so I think the most important element is the seeking itself.

Russell: Is the what?

Bentinho: Is the seeking itself; the will to seek, the desire. That will then attract all of the other tools needed.

Russell: What do you mean when you say, "You will find what you seek"?

Bentinho: You will always find the proof, the evidence and the conclusions that are commensurate with the level, or the nature, of what you're looking for. This is one of the inherent limitations (and beauties, if you can appreciate it from a distance) upon the path of the seeker of truth, or the seeker of God. We will always find "proof" to confirm our pre-existing notions.

For example, based on what you said earlier, St. Augustine was raised as a hardcore Christian and then later fully converted by his own will. From within that paradigm, he was trying to prove something logically, which has its limitations. He started with a belief, and rather than try to find the truth nakedly, without bias, he simply sought to prove what he already thought. This can be very interesting to the world he is writing for, and it can help to expand or ground or complete that paradigm, but it is no longer a desire for the *truth*; it is a desire for *proof*, right? There is a vast difference.

Russell: Exactly.

Bentinho: When the desire for truth becomes strong in a consciousness, in an individual, then all these other levels of intelligence begin to operate, begin to activate and move inside the body, the nervous system, and the brain; but also in my understanding, beyond that. The more metaphysical or spiritual components of one's intelligence, of one's capacity, begin to open up or activate.

The brain is the conduit, or the receiver (like a radio tuner), but it's not the originator of consciousness or knowledge. In my opinion, the brain receives insight and different perceptions of consciousness, and then translates that into imagery, activity, linearity and understanding. But it is not the *source* of it; it is the radio—the translator.

To me, the source of any type of insight or perception can most closely be compared to the ethers, or the frequencies that a radio tunes into. I see the brain as a "resonating chamber" that can be used to tune into certain perceptions or truths and receive "downloads" of truths and convert them into imagery and insights and understandings and perspectives that are commensurate with the frequency that one is tuned into. But the map is not the territory...

The song, as you hear it coming out of the radio (or translator), doesn't actually exist in the ethers; it exists as vibration, as information. Once the radio tunes into it and does what it is designed to do, it becomes music, it becomes a representation, or an explanation, of that frequency; it becomes an image of that frequency. It becomes something that the senses can hear.

Similarly, I think the brain operates as a receiver of universal data or knowledge. The ethers or vibrations exist whether or not the radio is turned on or is even created. In the same way, the truth exists before and beyond the brain, and whether or not the brain is dialed into the possibility of translating the truth. The truth is not the image that the brain presents.

What if there is a way to directly perceive, know, experience or even be the frequencies themselves, rather than be limited to the song that is produced by the radio or translator? Similarly, what if we can access higher levels of truth directly, and even "become" them (or remember that we already are them), instead of just perceiving ourselves through the intellect and the senses? Wouldn't you much prefer direct knowledge or experience over indirect, or translated, knowledge or experience?

I think that, inherent in all this, is that all universal knowledge exists in any and every portion of the Creation, because it is holographic in nature. When we use our individual bodies and brains, and our personal consciousness, to tune into things beyond the limits of what we see, we can access these other frequencies. And we are able to give symbolic representation to them in words.

Words are not the actual frequency; they are not the truth. They are the human interpretation of the truth or of these frequencies. Therefore, there will always be some distortion as soon as truth is spoken, written down, or drawn on a piece of paper. It is going to be distorted, it is going to be representative; it is not going to be the actual thing. Words are the map, not the territory itself. However, the map can be used to navigate the actual territory. This is what all genuine spiritual teaching is all about.

The most we can ever do with words is point to the truth. You can directly experience the truth, but as soon as you translate the truth to me, the words and the images and my interpretation of it are just functioning as pointers. It's like saying, "Dial your brain to 106 FM," but you must download music yourself.

Maybe I got a little off topic, but... yes! We have other avenues of knowing things and experiencing things that can sometimes open up for people. Meditation can definitely open this up for people, and just the sheer desire to seek beyond the known can open it up. If the desire is not greater than the complacency or okayness with our current understanding, those new avenues will most likely not be activated, except accidentally or by what religious people call "grace" perhaps. By God's grace, through some kind of incident or accident or coincidence, or due to some kind of handicap, physical disease, or terminal illness, or some sudden vision, near death experience, or spontaneous insight... people start seeking for a more spiritually-sound or complete perspective.

Russell: I have a few questions, if I can remember them all. I appreciate the concept of this knowledge coming in, which is non-verbal, perhaps even non-symbolic, which has to be translated if we want to talk about it with each other.

Bentinho: Yes, we have to give it symbolization.

Russell: Right. And something is always lost...

Bentinho: This is just a side note, but there are differences in how we choose to use symbolization. I am aware of the distortion that is inherent in symbolizing something that is known directly—it becomes more indirect. It becomes religious. It becomes a symbol. A distortion. There is a direct perspective, perception or experience, and I am making it less direct through symbolization, words and images. I distort it. I have to if I wish to use words and symbols. Now, I can share these symbolizations or distortions with another entity, with or without the conscious intention for them to be able to use it as a pointer to then tune-in themselves so they can have the same direct experience.

This is like Neo coming into the matrix (again, to use the analogy of *The Matrix*). Morpheus asks Neo before he wakes up, "Do you want to know what the matrix is?" He talks about the matrix using pointers to try to hint at the truth. He also says: "Unfortunately, no one can be told what the matrix is. You have to see it for yourself."

As an alternative to using pointers consciously and with the intention to aid another in using these pointers to access the truth for themselves, one can also simply express what is known directly, with no regard for its intended usage. I think this is sometimes the fault of religion—it's laid out there as a truth; it is not used as a tool for each individual to then, from within their own sovereignty, independently realize their connection to God and their ability to contact this God or Wholeness.

Russell: So, the understanding that you are directly receiving, which you are translating for me and for other people, do you feel that this core understanding is the same or similar to, say, Buddhism? Or maybe even parts of Christianity or other spiritual traditions?

Bentinho: For sure. I think a lot of religions share certain essences in their understanding, but it has become lost in translation, interpretation and symbolization. And then people start fighting over the symbols and images, rather than using them as pointers to realize the experiential truth directly.

But if you can see through the symbols and read into the original transcript inside of the scripture—if you can tune into what this original source was actually trying to explain, if you have awareness and will and you're not too lost—you can read between the lines and get a much more direct sense of how religious texts can be used as pointers. Then it becomes more experiential and more independently useful to each entity. It becomes less of a doctrine that exists outside of oneself and more of a science explaining how to gain that inner knowledge.

Russell: So, individuals should sort of translate it for themselves.

Bentinho: They already always do; there is no way around it. I might translate a certain realization for you, which is already a distortion, but then you translate my translation in a way that makes sense to you, from a place or paradigm that you are already familiar with. This is the great challenge for any genuine teacher—"genuine" meaning a teacher who is most sincere in their efforts to make their message understandable to those who hear it, with as little distortion as possible.

This is what distinguishes the master teachers of all times from many other wise men and women and philosophers, or perhaps simpler teachers. What makes the master teacher a great teacher, among several things, is the ability to quickly know the world of their student or audience, to a point where they can accurately estimate how they will translate (and necessarily distort) the message into words or symbols.

As a result of being aware of the student's tunnel of distortions that their own translation will have to pass through, master teachers can modify what they say to fit the filters of the student. They can predict with a high degree of accuracy how the given words will be interpreted and finally land in the conscious and subconscious mind of the listener.

The intention of the genuine teacher (or "guru" if you will) is, again, to provide the listener with an interpretation that is as close a translation as possible to the experience he or she is attempting to convey. Whereas a simpler teacher simply translates the experience according to their own set of symbols, the master teacher does not speak the words he or she prefers or is most familiar with per se, but rather deals directly with the interpretations and filters of the listener and adjusts his or her message accordingly.

This requires a great selflessness. Selflessness is another quality that separates the common teacher from the master teacher: the degree of their selflessness and their willingness to sacrifice their own image, words and preferences for the sake of the message landing in a valuable way for each student. Think about it... isn't the genuine purpose of teaching for the student to get the message? If a teacher simply toots his own horn or speaks his own language, then who is he really doing the teaching for—the student or himself?

This is also the reason why the words a master teacher utters are not necessarily reflections of the master's experience or point of view; they are more directly tools reflecting the state of the student. Because anything a master teacher or "mirror being" utters, is uttered for the sake of the listener and has therefore already been modified! So, the words are not directly a representation of the master teacher's own identity. However, the student will often mistake the words of the master for the opinions, preferences, identity or beliefs of the master. This is not always (in fact it is rarely) the case for a master teacher. One of these master teachers from our recent past, Ramana Maharshi (1879-1950), said it beautifully:

The sage's pure mind, which beholds as a mere witness the whole world, is like a mirror which reflects the foolish thoughts of those who come before him. And these thoughts are then mistaken to be his.

This attempt to tailor the message to have the most impact on the student is made more challenging for great teachers nowadays because of the internet. The benefit of our current age is that the message can immediately reach many more people. The downside is that the message will be distorted and misinterpreted in many more ways than it used to be, and to accurately tailor it to an audience has become more difficult.

In today's world, everyone can hear everything you're saying, and people often associate what the master teacher says with the master's own opinion or beingness. One on one teaching is easy, you see, because the master can tailor their message specifically to the student in front of him. But if the whole world is watching a dialogue that was specifically tailored to just one student, there will be highly varied and distorted translations of the message, because other viewers' filter-tunnels are different than those of the student for whom the message was designed.

So nowadays, master teachers have to jump through a lot more mental loops and make certain concessions in their messaging. They have to be aware of their entire audience. This complicates and necessarily further distorts the message. However, in my opinion, it is still better than no message, and it can be done to a satisfactory degree.

The master teacher, or mirror being, is someone who is

sensitive enough that they can even get a fairly precise read on the collective's filters as a whole and provide a message that will pass fairly undistorted through most filters. Of course, there are always severely biased people whom you cannot account for. These people will gravely misinterpret the message, no matter how it is worded. The message is simply not yet directly for them, even though they may be exposed to it.

The master teacher has to accept that their true message, their own experience, and their apparent identity—which by the way, are all the same thing in the accomplished master (their beingness or identity *is* their message)—will be greatly misunderstood. Being understood by others is simply not one of the privileges of a great and sincere teacher; being adored by some and attacked by others is more likely the outcome. This is one of the reasons that some great teachers, and also some of the simpler teachers, decide at one point or another to either stay silent, or to only teach to small and dedicated audiences. It is ever a tempting alternative to speaking publicly for all to hear and distort. Both have their benefits.

Russell: Yeah.

Bentinho: To get back to your question (whether or not individuals can translate religious scriptures for themselves), I would say in an ideal world this would be the case, but it is an unrealistic assumption in some ways. The most direct and realistic solution to preventing further distortions lies not with the listener so much, but rather with the disseminator or teacher. The listener cannot be expected to understand; otherwise they would not be the listener or student.

It's not that one is a victim and the other is a perpetrator, but if you want to correct some of these heavily distorted expressions you see in religion, you must correct it as close to the source as possible to have a beneficial influence. Ideally, the student becomes a better listener, but this simply cannot be expected. Just like you cannot expect a four-year-old child to understand advanced accounting. The best you can do is try to tailor your explanations to their level of understanding, and up-level or mature their understanding one step at a time.

Russell: Right; I see. You also talked about how, for people to seek this understanding, this universal consciousness, they really need the will to do so. It's part of the criteria.

Bentinho: Yes. By the way, have I mentioned yet that it's extremely blissful and rewarding to gain such understandings?

Russell: No, not today...

Bentinho: It's extremely worthwhile as a means to gain a deep sense of fulfillment—even for that alone; truth aside. And truth has always been very valuable to me; it has been a main component of my search. If you asked me in my earlier seeking years, and still today, "Would you rather be happy or would you rather know the truth?" I would choose the truth. But I've actually found them to be the same thing.

So yeah, the truth is blissful! The more undistorted we become in our perception of our own existence, of is-ness, the happier we are. I've found happiness and truth to be directly proportional to each other. It's noteworthy, I think, that the personal search for fulfillment and the (sort of) objective search for truth are understood to coincide.

Russell: I think that ties in well with my next question or sphere of inquiry.

Bentinho: How intuitive of you!

Russell: You've talked about how people who are happy in this material world are perhaps not as motivated, or don't have the will to seek this higher consciousness.

Bentinho: Yes.

Russell: My take on this material world is that it's real, that it's true, and your take is that there is a higher truth, and that this material world is an illusion. Is that fair to say?

Bentinho: It's difficult to use that word, but yes. There isn't a much better word for it.

Russell D.: Which word do you mean? Truth?

Bentinho: No, "higher." I usually try to avoid the words "higher and lower," but there is also some accuracy in those terms. You could also say "more whole" or "more inclusive." Because the higher you go, it's like what you were saying about the dialectic approach—instead of looking at just one component, you step back and see all components. Your perspective is still a perception, it's still an angle, but it now includes more points of data, and therefore, there is less paradox. Right? So we can use "higher" in that sense.

Russell: Or "larger"?

Bentinho: Yeah, larger, more all encompassing, more inclusive.

I would state that my view includes your view, while your view excludes my view. Without intending to sound arrogant, for the sake of clarifying some dynamics of this dialogue, I would say that I have a more inclusive perspective than you do, because I agree with everything you are saying, and I can see what level of consciousness it is coming from, but I am no longer bound by that paradigm alone. I have more resources to draw perspective from at this stage.

I don't disagree with your perceptions from that level; they are accurate observations. But I feel that I see more data points than you do, so I feel that I comprehend your paradigm, but I don't feel that you comprehend my paradigm. Just like a three-dimensional life form can understand the trajectory, paradigm and limitations of a two-dimensional life form quite well, while also having access to a broader perspective.

Russell: I want to explore that. In my view, this world is truth and there is not a universal consciousness.

Bentinho: Is this hypothetical or is it currently your stance?

Russell: That's my view.

Bentinho: OK, nice.

Russell: In your view, there is a universal consciousness and this world is an illusion.

Bentinho: Yes. The world is perception-based; it's not an independently existent system.

Russell: In my view, if someone is happy in this world, then they are happy. Now if someone is not happy in this world, they may have the choice to either try to become happy in this world (which will take effort), or they could take your perspective, your belief, your knowledge, that this is all an illusion. So, people who are unhappy in this world have more of a will, I would think, to seek the universal consciousness and to conceive of this world as an illusion. Is that true?

Bentinho: Generally speaking, yes, although it's always on a case by case basis. Going general implies a loss of precision, but in general I can loosely agree.

Russell: So, do you think that your followers tend to be more unhappy in this world than average?

Bentinho: At the initial point of starting their search, I cannot say that they are necessarily more unhappy over-all, but they may typically be more unhappy with the world they seem to find themselves in, yes. Now, they can become much happier than the average person through their process, through their discovery and with the tools that are provided, and often they do. But the initial point that gets them to ask questions and seek... well, there is a lot of complexity to this question. It cannot truly be answered with a blanket statement, but typically there is some degree of discontentment with the world they perceive through their mind and senses.

Russell: I think there are some people who are just curious.

Bentinho: Exactly. Something from within drives them, even if they are already happier than the average Joe who lacks this same level of drive to seek the truth. Let's say there are simply some who have less tolerance for, or find less satisfaction in, the way things are seemingly set up around them. And this can translate into frustration or depression.

Someone else might not be super happy on the vibrational scale of bliss, but they may be very tolerant and okay with their understanding of the way things are. They may not intuitively remember something better is possible. They might not experience as much of a vibrational discrepancy between who they feel or believe they are and what they observe on a day to day basis in this societal collective consciousness and what is agreed upon therein. It's more agreeable to them.

So yeah, it can often translate as being less happy on the surface level. But I have often experienced great happiness and frustration simultaneously, because of my intolerance of the limitations of our understanding and the consequent actions of our society, which seem insane to me in some ways. There is an intuitive sense within me that feels we live in an insane asylum of our own creation in many ways. My frustration or disagreement with this didn't always necessarily mean being unhappy, because at the same time, there was a great sense of purposefulness in seeking for more and knowing that there is more.

Now, if someone observes the world around them with a sense of disagreement and a strong intuitive sense of, "This makes no sense," but they don't believe they can find a deeper truth and meaning, then they would be unhappy.

Russell: Right, because they don't believe they can do anything about it. But you felt like you could.

Bentinho: Yes, I've always felt like I could; I've always felt that the answers are somehow within my capacity to know. So, I wouldn't say that I was more unhappy than the average Joe; I would actually say that I have always felt more alive, more vibrant.

Russell: You took it as a challenge.

Bentinho: In a sense, yeah, it was more of a challenge. I just needed to know. It was a deep yearning; there was a deep desire for it and a knowingness and trust in the possibility of liberation.

Russell: You had a sense, or an intuition, or a belief that

you could find the answers. That's cool.

Bentinho: That's why I really wasn't unhappy. I had periods of depression, emotional devastation, turmoil, confusion, and even existential angst, but I would still say that I have been happier, or felt more alive, than the average Joe overall, including in my earlier years. Even considering those who are more tolerant about the way things are understood to be.

And I think there is a beauty sometimes (not always but sometimes) with people just being completely OK with what they know and not seeking any greater knowing. I don't recommend it overall, but sometimes I think it can really suit a particular person. But it's rare. It usually doesn't look too good on a person, from where I stand. It usually feels like they are simply asleep. Like the walking dead. But there are cases where it just really suits that person; it's perfect for where they are at, and there is a radiance and peacefulness about them. And I really appreciate seeing that, though it is rare.

Russell: Are you talking about someone who is happy but not spiritual?

Bentinho: Not consciously spiritual perhaps, yes. I would not generally classify them as truly happy, but rather as content, peaceful, in acceptance, having sort of a mastery of themselves, integrated, having come to terms with who they are in this world. The ideal grandfather or grandmother. There is a beauty to that, and there is a certain happiness and radiance with these people.

But typically, people are not very satisfied. I think you are somewhat of an exception; I think it looks better on you than it does on most people who share your views. I think you have settled into it quite nicely, and so it suits you. It's where you're at and there is a desire to learn and grow and expand, but without any sense of disastrous urgency or frustration. So you're not fully asleep and therefore perhaps don't fit the category of people we are discussing. That's how it seems to me, anyway. So, you carry it well. You carry suffering well. [Laughter]

So, there you go! You are one of the more content people with being unhappy that I know.

Russell: Hahaha!

Bentinho: These are all compliments, by the way.

Russell: Ignorance is bliss, right?

Bentinho: Well, yeah; there is some truth to that. "The stick bends in the water! Yeah! Look how beautifully bent it is! I never knew that water bends a stick, but it does! I feel great!"

Russell: Everytime! And then it lets it go. It's magic!

Bentinho: And I didn't mean to be offensive; I was joking around with you. You know that.

Russell: I don't think you were joking and I don't think you were offensive.

Bentinho: OK, then.

Russell: I am a little bit hard to offend.

Bentinho: Yeah, that's nice.

ABOUT THE AUTHOR

Born in Amsterdam in 1988, Bentinho Massaro is a spiritual teacher and author who hosts events and retreats in major US and European cities, as well as offers a number of online training programs (see *Resources*). With a significant internet presence, Bentinho has been inspiring a large global online community for several years, offering spiritual guidance to all who seek freedom and who wish to dedicate their lives to the service of others and to the planet as a whole.

Known for the precision of his teachings and his edgy, irreverent style, Bentinho is the leading synthesizer of enlightenment and empowerment teachings, resolving paradoxes and unifying the essence of seemingly divergent paths, both ancient and modern. He presents this as a unified teaching platform to our modern, collective world in ways that allow the "average Joe" to directly experience these metaphysical truths and higher states of consciousness. Bentinho continues to refine his teachings, with the goal of reaching people from every walk of life, building a bridge to enlightenment and self-empowerment for everyone.

Besides teaching and writing, Bentinho has taken on additional roles as entrepreneur, inventor, innovator and investor, exploring new ways to help this planet achieve balance and harmony, and to give the people a fair chance to wake up from their dream of illusory separateness. His desire is for the whole of this planet to become a thriving, spiritually-conducive playground for future generations.

RESOURCES

Stay connected! To learn more about Bentinho, his teachings, and his current offerings and programs, check out the webpages below.

BentinhoMassaro.com: Bentinho's main website offers a good introduction to Bentinho and his work. Read his blog articles, sign up for his newsletter, and keep up to date on his latest events.

BentinhoMassaro.com/Offerings: A complete listing of all of Bentinho's current offerings, all in one place, including descriptions and links.

TrinfinityAcademy.com: If you are new to Bentinho's teachings, we recommend you start with Trinfinity Academy, Bentinho's free online academy, in which he presents the basics of Enlightenment, Empowerment and Infinity.

BentinhoMassaro.tv: A monthly subscription membership offering over 800 hours of videos and audios of Bentinho's most recent events.

CivilizationUpgraders.com: Bentinho offers two cutting-edge online teaching programs under the Civilization Upgraders brand—Shepherding Consciousness and The Next Level.

You can also follow Bentinho on social media:

Instagram.com/BentinhoMassaro: Bentinho's preferred social media platform.

Facebook.com/BentinhoMassaro: Bentinho's public Facebook page. Also search for *Bentinho Massaro's Teaching and Community* to join his online community Facebook group.

YouTube.com/BentinhoMassaro: View over 400 of Bentinho's videos for free on YouTube.